THE CHRISTMAS COOKBOOK

Contents

Foreword

When I got married I couldn't cook; in fact I even
managed to burn a boiled egg – no mean achievement!
Since that inauspicious beginning I have become
fascinated with cooking. My method of learning has
always been trial and error: I like breaking the rules, I like
adding to, altering and doing my own thing to recipes.
I'd like to think you will do just that to my own recipes in
this book.

What I hope to present to you are the dishes I enjoy
most – my favourites for this, my favourite, time of the
year, Christmas.

Christmas Note

If you are one of those people who are completely organised – plan everything weeks ahead, make lists, do your Christmas shopping during the January sales, send Christmas cards early, deep freeze meals for the masses, spend Christmas day looking cool and collected – or, alternatively, if you loathe Christmas and go to any lengths to avoid any part of it, then don't buy this book! Put it back on the shelves immediately and save your money.

If, however, you are like me and my family and you enjoy Christmas and are fortunate enough to have friends and loved ones who gather round at the festive season, but at the same time wouldn't mind a few new ideas, some extra recipes, a fresh slant on old customs, a less-than-jaundiced look at some original suggestions to make your Christmas a memorable occasion, then buy this book quickly. You've made the right choice – start looking forward to it because you are going to have a very merry Christmas.

It's people who make Christmas
Everything else is a plus . . .
Here in this book are a
few of my own personal plusses –
I hope you enjoy them

Good Beginnings

The following recipes are starters — the first course for the traditional three course meal — should you feel like breaking with tradition, then use these ideas as lunch or supper dishes and start your dinner with the main attraction.
For lunch or supper, these recipes will save you time (and maybe your sanity!) during the frantic holiday season. So, although the choice of how you use them is yours, we'll start at the beginning. . . .

Split Pea Soup

450 g/1 lb split peas · 1 ham bone
2 large onions, cut in chunks
1 cooking apple, peeled, cored and chopped
3.5 litres/6 pints water
salt and pepper

Soak the split peas for 1 hour, then drain and rinse them and remove any odd looking specimens. Put the peas in a large saucepan with all the other ingredients. Bring to the boil, reduce the heat and simmer, covered, until tender – about 1 hour. Skim the soup occasionally.

When the peas are soft, remove the ham bone and add seasoning to taste. Blend the soup in batches in a liquidiser or food processor and reheat before serving. **Serves 8**

Curried Parsnip Soup

40 g/1½ oz butter
2 onions, chopped
2 teaspoons peeled and chopped fresh root ginger
¼ teaspoon ground coriander
generous pinch each of cayenne pepper, turmeric,
ground cumin and nutmeg
450 g/1 lb parsnips, peeled and chopped
1 medium potato, peeled and chopped
1 litre/1¾ pints chicken stock
salt
curry powder (optional)
150 ml/¼ pint soured cream

Melt the butter in a large saucepan. Add the chopped onions and cook gently until very soft but not browned. Stir in the ginger and spices, then fry for 1 minute, stirring constantly. Stir in the parsnips and potatoes and continue to stir-fry for a minute. Pour in the stock, give the soup a stir, then bring to the boil. Cover the pan and simmer gently until the vegetables are soft – about 45 minutes.

Blend the cooked soup until smooth in batches in a liquidiser, and return it to the pan. Reheat the soup thoroughly and taste for seasoning, adding a little salt or curry powder as necessary, then stir in the cream. Serve very hot. This soup freezes well. **Serves 6**

Carrot Soup

50 g/2 oz butter
2 medium onions, finely chopped
2 sticks celery, finely chopped
1 kg/2 lb carrots, thinly sliced
2 medium potatoes, thinly sliced
600 ml/1 pint chicken stock
1 teaspoon sugar
salt and pepper
300 ml/½ pint milk
300 ml/½ pint double cream
GARNISH
chopped fresh mint
grated carrot

Melt the butter in a saucepan, add the chopped onions and celery and sauté until the vegetables are soft but not brown. Add the sliced carrots and potatoes and quickly toss these in the butter with the other vegetables. Pour in the chicken stock then stir in the sugar and seasoning to taste. Bring the soup to the boil, turn down the heat and simmer gently for about 15 minutes or until the carrots are soft.

Pour batches of the soup into a liquidiser or food processor and purée the ingredients until smooth. Allow the soup to cool, then chill it thoroughly. Stir in the milk and cream and re-chill the soup. Serve, garnished with chopped mint and grated carrot.

Alternatively, to serve hot, reheat the soup gently making sure that it does not boil (or the cream will curdle) and serve topped with a little extra cream. **Serves 6 to 8**

Quick Creamed Broccoli Soup

2 (227-g/8-oz) packets frozen broccoli
1.15 litres/2 pints chicken stock
1 onion, chopped
2 sticks celery, chopped
salt and pepper
300 ml/½ pint double cream

Put the broccoli in a saucepan with the stock, chopped onion and celery; bring to the boil, then lower the heat, cover and simmer for 10 minutes.

Blend the soup in batches, in a liquidiser or food processor, until smooth. Return the soup to the saucepan. Season to taste, add the cream and mix thoroughly. Reheat slowly without allowing the soup to boil, then serve with croûtons (neat cubes of bread, fried in a mixture of butter and oil until crisp and golden). **Serves 8**

Note: Watercress can be used in this recipe instead of the broccoli. Use 2 bunches watercress, trimmed, and prepare the soup as above. Chill the purée before stirring in the cream and serve the cold soup garnished with sprigs of watercress.

Desperate Quick Soup

50 g/2 oz butter
2 onions, chopped
2 sticks celery, chopped
750 ml/1¼ pints chicken stock
1 (225-g/8-oz) packet frozen peas
1 tablespoon chopped fresh mint
150 ml/¼ pint single cream (optional)

Melt the butter in a saucepan, add the chopped onions and celery and cook over a moderate heat until soft – about 8 minutes. Add the chicken stock and peas, then bring to the boil and simmer for 10 minutes. Leave to cool.

This soup can be served hot or cold, garnished with the chopped mint. To serve it cold, add the cream (if used) and chill the soup. Alternatively reheat the soup, then add the cream just before serving, but do not allow the soup to boil. **Serves 4 to 6.**

Consommé with Soured Cream and Caviar

(Illustrated on pages 26/27)

2 (411-g/14½-oz) cans Crosse and Blackwell beef consommé
150 ml/¼ pint soured cream
1 (99-g/3½-oz) jar caviar or lumpfish roe
lemon slices to garnish

Pour the consommé into five or six wide-necked glasses and place them in the refrigerator until set – 3 to 4 hours. Alternatively, chill the soup in one large bowl until set, then spoon it into the glasses.

Top each portion with a little soured cream and a spoonful of caviar or lumpfish roe. Garnish with lemon slices and serve ice-cold. Hand hot toast separately, or serve with herbed bread. **Serves 5 to 6**

Chop two or three of your favourite herbs to make herb bread. Mix about a handful of each with softened butter. Slice a french loaf diagonally, leaving the slices attached at the base, then butter them and press the loaf back together. Top with sprigs of fresh herbs and pack the loaf in cooking foil, then bake in a moderately hot oven (190 C, 375 F, gas 5) for 15 to 20 minutes.

Consommé with Cream Cheese

Dissolve 7g/¼oz gelatine in 1 tablespoon warmed sherry. Blend this mixture with 2 (411-g/14½-oz) cans consommé in a liquidiser. Reserve a quarter of the comsommé for the topping, then blend the remaining soup with 275 g/10 oz Philadelphia cream cheese. Pour into six individual wide-necked glasses and chill until set. Dissolve the reserved consommé but do not allow it to become too hot, then pour a thin layer over the soup in each glass. Return to the refrigerator until the consommé has set. Serve with hot toast. **Serves 6**

Smoked Salmon and Watercress Mousse

(Illustrated on page 25)

Fresh or frozen smoked salmon trimmings can be bought at a discount from delicatessens and supermarkets.

350 g/12 oz smoked salmon pieces
350 g/12 oz cottage cheese
150 ml/$\frac{1}{4}$ pint soured cream
2 tablespoons lemon juice
salt and pepper
cayenne pepper
4 bunches watercress
2 tablespoons mayonnaise
GARNISH
curls of smoked salmon
sprigs of watercress
lemon slices

Roughly chop the smoked salmon, then put the pieces into a liquidiser or food processor with 100 g/4 oz of the cottage cheese, the soured cream and lemon juice (you may need to do this in several batches). Process until smooth and season to taste with salt and cayenne. Tip the purée into a bowl.

Pick all the leaves off the watercress and discard the stalks. Plunge the leaves into boiling water for 10 seconds. Drain, rinse with cold water, then drain thoroughly, squeezing out the excess liquid. Blend the watercress with the remaining cottage cheese and mayonnaise in a liquidiser or food processor until smooth. Season with salt and pepper.

Pour a third of the salmon mixture into a glass serving bowl. Cover with half the watercress mixture. Repeat, then top with a layer of the salmon mixture. Cover and chill until ready to serve.

If you wish, the mousse can be decorated with curls of smoked salmon, sprigs of watercress and lemon slices. Serve with crisp wholewheat rolls or toast. **Serves 4 to 6**

Shrimp and Sherry Starter

1 medium onion, finely chopped
75 g/3 oz butter
6 canned tomatoes, drained and chopped
6 mushrooms, chopped
6 (100-g/4-oz) cartons potted shrimps
2 tablespoons double cream
dash of sherry
6 slices white bread, with crusts removed
1 tablespoon oil
chopped parsley to garnish

Sauté the finely chopped onion in half the butter until soft – about 5 minutes. Add the tomatoes and mushrooms and stir for a minute over a moderate heat. Next stir in the potted shrimps, cream and a good dash of sherry and warm through gently.

Fry the bread slices in the remaining butter and the oil, turning them once, until golden brown on both sides. Top the bread with the shrimp mixture and serve immediately, garnished with chopped parsley. **Serves 6**

Fish Terrine

You could make this and give it in a pretty dish as a useful early gift to someone who is going to be too busy to cook over Christmas.

225 g/8 oz cooked salmon, kippers, smoked haddock, fresh or
smoked trout, or smoked mackerel
3 canned anchovy fillets, drained
100 g/4 oz unsalted butter, softened
a little lemon juice
cayenne pepper
75 g/3 oz butter, melted for topping

Blend all the ingredients together in a food processor or mash them with a fork and beat until smooth. Taste for seasoning and adjust it if necessary by adding more lemon juice or cayenne. Press the pâté into ramekins or one large dish and pour the melted butter over to form a seal. Chill until firm. Serve with hot toast. **Serves 6**

Egg and Asparagus Starter

1 (340-g/12-oz) can asparagus tips, drained
6 hard-boiled eggs
6 tablespoons double cream
salt and pepper
100 g/4 oz grated cheese
50 g/2 oz chopped salted peanuts

Place four or five asparagus tips in each of six individual ovenproof ramekins or small dishes. Quarter the eggs lengthways and arrange the pieces in neat rows on top of the asparagus, white side up. Pour a tablespoonful of cream over each of the eggs. Season, then sprinkle with grated cheese and chopped peanuts.

Place the ramekins in a moderately hot oven (190 c, 375 f, gas 5) for 5 to 10 minutes, or until the top is lightly browned (care must be taken not to overcook this dish). Serve immediately. **Serves 6**

Stuffed Pasta Shells

225 g/8 oz large pasta shells
350 g/12 oz cottage cheese
2 eggs
1 onion, finely chopped
$\frac{1}{2}$ green pepper, deseeded and finely chopped
1 (198-g/7-oz) can tuna, drained
100 ml/4 fl oz double cream
25 g/1 oz butter
25 g/1 oz fresh breadcrumbs

Bring a large saucepan of salted water to the boil, add the pasta shells and simmer gently for about 8 minutes, or until the pasta is just tender. Drain, rinse in cold water and drain thoroughly.

Mix all the remaining ingredients together apart from the butter and breadcrumbs. Carefully fill the shells with the cottage cheese mixture and place them in a greased baking dish. Dot with butter and sprinkle with breadcrumbs. Cover with cooking foil and bake in a moderate oven (180 c, 350 f, gas 4) for 25 minutes

At the end of the cooking time remove the foil covering and brown the stuffed pasta under the grill. Serve immediately. **Serves 4 to 6**

Special Macaroni Cheese

225 g/8 oz macaroni
65 g/2½ oz butter
40 g/1½ oz flour
450 ml/¾ pint milk
100 g/4 oz lean cooked ham, cut into strips
4 large tomatoes, peeled and chopped
175 g/6 oz cheese, grated
salt and pepper
2 tablespoons fresh breadcrumbs

Cook the macaroni in plenty of simmering, salted water for 10 to 12 minutes or until just tender, then drain.

Meanwhile, place 40 g/1½ oz of the butter, the flour and milk in a saucepan and cook over a low heat, whisking continuously, until the sauce boils and thickens. Let the sauce simmer for a few minutes to make sure the flour is cooked.

Stir the macaroni, ham, tomatoes and 100 g/4 oz of the cheese into the sauce, then continue stirring until the cheese has completely melted. Season well. Transfer to buttered individual ovenproof dishes. Mix the remaining cheese with the breadcrumbs and sprinkle over the top of the macaroni. Dot the surface with the remaining butter and bake in a moderately hot oven (200 C, 400 F, gas 6) for 20 minutes or until the cheese topping is crisp and golden. Serve immediately. **Serves 6**

Pâté in Brioche

FOR EACH SERVING ALLOW:
1 brioche
15 g/½ oz softened butter
about 40 g/1½ oz pâté
shredded lettuce or watercress to serve

Cut the cap off the brioche and scoop out the soft crumb from the centre. Spread the inside with the softened butter and heat in a moderate oven (180 C, 350 F, gas 4) until crisp – about 10 minutes.

Fill with your favourite pâté and replace the cap. Serve on a bed of shredded lettuce or watercress.

Chicken Pâté

450 g/1 lb breast of chicken, skinned and roughly chopped
2 egg whites
4 tablespoons double cream
450 g/1 lb broccoli, cooked and puréed
salt and pepper
salad ingredients to garnish;
for example cucumber, radishes and tomatoes

Purée chicken in a liquidiser or food processor. Add the egg whites and half the cream and blend until smooth. Stir the broccoli purée into the mixture, adding salt and pepper to taste. Fold in rest of the cream.

Pour the pâté into a suitable ovenproof serving dish. Cover the dish and stand it in a large roasting tin. Pour in hot water to come halfway up the side of the dish. Cover with cooking foil and cook in a moderate oven (160 c, 325 f, gas 3) for 1½ hours. Cool and chill overnight.

Turn out on to a platter and serve, garnished with salad ingredients of your choice. **Serves 6**

Bloody Mary Starter

juice of 2 lemons · 250 ml/8 fl oz tomato juice
3 tablespoons vodka · pinch of salt
a few drops of Worcestershire sauce (or to taste)
freshly ground black pepper
1 egg white · 4 ice cubes, crushed
lemon slices to decorate

Place all the ingredients in a liquidiser or food processor and blend until frothy. Pour into a suitable container and put in the freezer. After 30 minutes give the mixture a good stir, then cover and return the container to the freezer and leave until the mixture is solid.

To serve, transfer the container to the refrigerator for 30 minutes. Spoon into chilled cocktail or wine glasses and decorate with lemon slices. **Serves 4**

Avocado Starter

(Illustrated on pages 26/27)

3 ripe avocado pears
3 sticks celery
3 spring onions (optional)
1 tart dessert apple
3 tablespoons mayonnaise
salt and pepper

Home-made mayonnaise is the nicest.

Cut the avocados in half and remove the stones. Scoop out the flesh, leaving the shell intact. Chop the flesh neatly. Cut the celery into matchsticks, and put these into ice cold water for a few minutes to crisp up. Slice the spring onions diagonally (if used) and add them to the chopped avocado. Quarter, core and dice the apple, then stir it into the avocado mixture with the drained celery and the mayonnaise. Season to taste. Spoon the mixture into the reserved avocado shells and serve immediately. **Serves 6**

Stuffed Whole Avocados

6 ripe avocado pears
2 tablespoons lemon juice
175 g/6 oz Philadelphia cream cheese
2 tablespoons chopped canned pimento
1 tablespoon finely chopped chives
salt and pepper
Tabasco sauce

This is an interesting way of serving avocados. I first had them at a dinner party given by Doreen Hawkins and she told me how to make them.

Cut the avocados in half across the middle (not lengthways). Twist the halves to separate them, then brush the cut surfaces with lemon juice to prevent discoloration. Carefully remove the avocado stones and brush the hollows with lemon juice.

Mix the Philadelphia cheese with the pimento and chives. Season to taste with salt, pepper and Tabasco, then stuff the avocados with this mixture by pressing the cheese into the holes left by the stones. Put the avocado halves back together and wrap each avocado in cling film. Chill until ready to eat.

Peel the avocados, then thinly slice them into rings. Arrange the slices on individual plates, then serve with Vinaigrette Dressing (page 61) and Quick Walnut Bread (page 83). **Serves 6**

Savoury Stuffed Pears

Walnut and Roquefort

(Illustrated on page 148)

4 large ripe pears
100 g/4 oz Roquefort cheese, mashed
50 g/2 oz chopped walnuts
3 tablespoons double cream, whipped
1 tablespoon brandy
25 g/1 oz walnuts, chopped
GARNISH
walnut halves
sprigs of watercress

Core the whole pears from the underneath, leaving their stalks in place. Mix the cheese with the chopped walnuts, cream and brandy, to make a creamy paste. Press this stuffing into the cavities from the cores, then serve one stuffed pear per person, garnished with walnut halves and watercress.

If preparing in advance, brush the pears with lemon juice to stop them from turning brown. Serve with Ginger Thins (page 118). **Serves 4**

Port and Stilton

4 large ripe pears, peeled and halved
100 g/4 oz ripe Stilton cheese
2 tablespoons port
2 tablespoons cream cheese
watercress to garnish

Core the pears. Mash the stilton with the port and cream cheese. Spoon this filling into the pears and garnish with watercress. **Serves 8**

Peculiar Fruit Salad

Select as many different fruits as possible – the more the better. Prepare
the fruit according to its type, then arrange it attractively on a large dish.
In a screw-topped jar, mix 3 tablespoons lemon juice, 2 tablespoons each
of sunflower oil and olive oil and seasoning to taste. Shake well and pour
this dressing over the fruit. Chill for 30 minutes before serving.

*When Bryan and I were making a film in Westport, Connecticut
we lived near an amazing market where you could buy the
most incredible fruits. I used to make this fruit salad as a
first course, as a dessert for pudding haters or with cottage
cheese for a diet lunch.*

Pineapple, Avocado and Yogurt Salad

1 ripe pineapple
1 ripe avocado pear, peeled, stoned and thinly sliced
small bunch of grapes, halved and stoned
50 g/2 oz pistachio nuts, shelled and chopped
300 ml/$\frac{1}{2}$ pint natural yogurt
2 teaspoons freshly chopped mint
1 small lettuce, shredded

Cut the pineapple in half lengthways. Cut out the flesh, remove the core
and chop the fruit into chunks. Mix the fruit with the avocado, grapes,
most of the pistachios, the yogurt and mint. Mix well and chill. Serve on
lettuce, garnished with the reserved nuts. **Serves 4**

Note: When very small pineapples are in the shops I serve one per
person. Slice the top off the pineapple, then scoop out and chop the flesh,
discarding the core. Mix the fruit with the other ingredients as above,
then spoon the salad back into the pineapple shells and replace the lids.
Decorate the top by placing fresh flowers in amongst the leaves.

Pepper and Anchovy Salad

1 (50-g/1¾-oz) can anchovy fillets
3 tablespoons olive oil
knob of butter
2 tablespoons double cream
6 red or green peppers

Pound the anchovies in a pestle and mortar or purée them until smooth. Heat 2 tablespoons of the oil and the butter in a small frying pan, add the anchovies and cook for a few minutes. Tip into a liquidiser, add the cream and blend until smooth.

Cut the tops off the peppers and remove all the seeds. Drop the peppers into a large pan of boiling water, adding the remaining oil, and simmer for 5 minutes.

Drain the peppers and arrange them on a serving dish, either whole, halved or sliced. Serve the fairly small amount of the rich anchovy sauce in a small bowl to accompany the peppers, and offer hot French bread as an accompaniment. **Serves 6**

Spiced Aubergine with Tomato

1 aubergine
3 tablespoons lemon juice
175 g/6 oz plain flour
1 egg
250 ml/8 fl oz milk
oil for frying
1 (397-g/14-oz) can chopped tomatoes
2 cloves garlic, crushed
salt and pepper
pinch of nutmeg
¼ teaspoon dried mixed herbs
2 teaspoons cider vinegar
1 teaspoon sugar
175 g/6 oz mozzarella cheese, grated

Slice the aubergine thinly and sprinkle the slices with lemon juice. Sift 100 g/4 oz of the flour into a bowl, make a well in the middle and add the egg. Gradually pour in the milk and beat thoroughly to make a smooth batter. Toss the aubergine slices in the rest of the flour, then dip them in the batter and shallow fry them for 2 minutes on each side or until golden. Remove the aubergine slices from the frying pan and drain them on absorbent kitchen paper.

Mix the tomatoes, garlic, seasoning, nutmeg, herbs, cider vinegar and sugar. Place half the aubergine slices into six individual ovenproof dishes or one large dish. Cover with a layer of the tomato mixture and mozzarella cheese, then top with a second layer of aubergines, the remaining tomatoes and finally top with the last of the cheese.

Place in a moderate oven (160 C, 325 F, gas 3) for 30 minutes or until the cheese is melted and lightly browned.

Serve with hot French bread. **Serves 6**

Cabbage Pie

$7\,g/\frac{1}{4}\,oz$ butter
about 12 (or more) Savoy cabbage leaves (depending on size)
$675\,g/1\frac{1}{2}\,lb$ cooked vegetables
(a mixture of as many of the following as you wish: sliced
carrots, sliced onions, sliced leeks, diced parsnips, sliced or
diced courgettes, roughly chopped spinach, sliced or chopped
cabbage, whole, diced or sliced green or runner beans, diced or
sliced potatoes, halved Brussels sprouts, peas, sliced green, red
or yellow peppers, sliced aubergines and sliced mushrooms)
salt and pepper · 4 eggs, lightly beaten
$100\,g/4\,oz$ Cheddar cheese, grated
$200\,ml/7\,fl\,oz$ single cream
2 tablespoons chopped parsley or chives

Butter a 25-cm/10-in quiche dish. Remove and discard the hard stalk from the leaves, then blanch them in boiling salted water for about 3 minutes or until just tender. Drain, rinse with cold water, then drain again thoroughly. Use these cabbage leaves to line the quiche dish, placing them so that they overlap the sides of the dish.

Put the cooked vegetables in a bowl and mix them thoroughly with seasoning to taste. Mix the eggs with the cheese and cream, stir in half the herbs and season to taste. Spoon the vegetable mixture into the lined quiche dish and pour over the egg mixture. Fold the cabbage leaves over the filling, using more cabbage leaves if necessary to completely cover the filling. Bake in a moderately hot oven (190 C, 375 F, gas 5) for about 30 minutes, or until golden and set. Sprinkle with the remaining herbs and serve hot, from the dish, or turn out. Served cold, this tastes equally as good. **Serves 6 to 8**

Small Quiches

250 g/9 oz plain flour
100 g/4 oz unsalted butter
2 egg yolks
generous pinch of salt
3–4 tablespoons cold water
100 g/4 oz rindless streaky bacon, chopped
freshly ground black pepper
grated nutmeg
350 g/12 oz frozen chopped spinach, defrosted and thoroughly
drained
225 g/8 oz cottage cheese
150 ml/$\frac{1}{4}$ pint double cream
3 eggs, beaten
2 tablespoons grated Parmesan or Gruyère cheese
8 rashers streaky bacon, rolled up and grilled, to garnish

Sift the flour into a large bowl, then rub in the butter until the mixture resembles fine breadcrumbs. Mix the egg yolks with the salt and 3 tablespoons water. Stir into the flour, using a knife, to make a soft and smooth – but not sticky – dough; add the extra water if the mixture is too dry. Wrap the dough in greaseproof paper and chill until firm.

Roll out the pastry on a floured surface and use to line 8 (7.5-cm/ $3\frac{1}{2}$-in) tartlet shells. Prick the pastry and bake blind in a hot oven (220 c, 425 f, gas 7) for 10 to 12 minutes. Remove from the oven and reduce the temperature to moderately hot (190 c, 375 f, gas 5).

Dry-fry the bacon over a high heat for 5 minutes, stirring constantly, then remove from the pan and season with black pepper and a little nutmeg to taste. Mix with the spinach, add the cottage cheese, cream and eggs and stir to mix thoroughly. Spoon into the pastry cases, sprinkle with grated cheese and bake in the heated oven for 15 minutes or until set. Garnish with bacon rolls and serve warm. **Serves 8**

Note: These are very useful because they can be a first course, a light lunch with salad, or to have with drinks as an after-theatre supper.

Opposite page Smoked Salmon and Watercress Mousse (page 14)
and Caesar Salad (page 57)
Overleaf Clockwise from the top left: Pineapple, Pepper and
Cottage Cheese Salad (page 60), Consommé with Soured Cream and
Caviar (page 13), Tomato and Mozzarella Salad (page 60) and
Avocado Starter (page 19)

The Main Event

The way you begin and end a meal is rather like
the first and last act of a play.
Act I: everyone seated, waiting and anticipating.
The last course is the final curtain, leaving the
audience — your guests — feeling that the evening
has been well spent. What happens in the middle
— The Main Event — is the heart of the matter.
    I have chosen the following recipes not only
because they taste wonderful for lunch or dinner
but also because, should you decide to break with
tradition (and why not?) and abandon the three
course habit, these Main Events will stand on
their own. Served with salad or vegetables, you
can forget your starter, have fruit and cheese
instead of a pudding and still receive rave
reviews from your friends.

Opposite page Christmas Goose with Potato Stuffing (page 34),
Yams in Orange Shells (page 53) and stuffing served in individual
dishes

Stuffed Lemon Sole
with White Wine Sauce

8 lemon sole fillets
1 (198–g/7–oz) can tuna or salmon, drained
50 g/2 oz Philadelphia cream cheese
4 tablespoons double cream
salt and pepper
150 ml/$\frac{1}{4}$ pint white wine
50 g/2 oz butter
25 g/1 oz flour
300 ml/$\frac{1}{2}$ pint milk
2 egg yolks
2 tablespoons lemon juice
1 tablespoon chopped parsley
parsley or watercress to garnish

Remove the black skin from the fish fillets. Put the tuna or salmon, Philadelphia cheese, 1 tablespoon cream and seasoning in a liquidiser or food processor and blend until smooth. Place a spoonful of this mixture on each fish fillet (on the skinned side) and roll up. Arrange the fish rolls in a greased ovenproof dish and pour in half the white wine, cover with buttered greaseproof paper and bake in a moderate oven (160 c, 325 f, gas 3) for 20 minutes. Transfer the fish to a warmed serving dish and keep hot.

Meanwhile, make the wine sauce by combining the butter, flour and milk in a saucepan. Heat until the sauce boils, whisking continuously, then add the cooking juices from the fish and the remaining wine; simmer for 2 minutes.

Take the saucepan off the heat and whisk in the egg yolks, lemon juice and remaining cream, then stir the sauce over a low heat, without allowing it to boil, until thickened. Stir in the chopped parsley and seasoning to taste.

Pour the sauce over the sole, garnish with parsley or watercress and serve immediately. **Serves 4**

Special-occasion Lobster

(Illustrated on pages 66/67)

Simple to make but with a luxurious taste. The lobster can be fresh, frozen or canned, or — if you wish — it can be replaced with cooked fresh salmon or cooked smoked haddock, but the result is somehow not quite the same!

450 g/1 lb cooked lobster meat
100 g/4 oz frozen peeled prawns, thawed
2 hard-boiled eggs, chopped
2 tomatoes, peeled, quartered, deseeded and diced
300 ml/$\frac{1}{2}$ pint mayonnaise
20 g/$\frac{3}{4}$ oz butter
20 g/$\frac{3}{4}$ oz flour
300 ml/$\frac{1}{2}$ pint milk
15 g/$\frac{1}{2}$ oz gelatine
2 tablespoons water
300 ml/$\frac{1}{2}$ pint double or whipping cream, whipped
salt and pepper
tomato ketchup, anchovy essence and lemon juice to taste
Garnish
cucumber slices
tomato slices
onion rings
whole shrimps
a little aspic jelly (optional)

Flake the lobster meat or chop it roughly and put it into a large bowl with the prawns, eggs, tomatoes and the mayonnaise

Melt the butter in a saucepan, stir in the flour, then gradually stir in the milk, Bring to the boil, stirring constantly, and simmer for 2 minutes. The sauce should be smooth and thick.

Dissolve the gelatine in the water in a basin over a saucepan of hot water, then stir it into the sauce. Leave the mixture to cool, stirring occasionally, but do not allow it to set. Mix the sauce into the lobster mixture with the cream. Add salt and pepper, tomato ketchup, anchovy essence and lemon juice to taste.

Spoon the mousse into a large glass serving bowl and chill until set. When set, garnish as wished with any of the suggested ingredients and spoon a little aspic jelly (if used) over the garnish. Chill again until ready to use. Serve with brown bread and butter. **Serves 6**

Christmas Turkey

(Illustrated on pages 46/47)

It goes without saying, that it is much better to buy a fresh turkey if you can, rather than a frozen one, as the flavour is much better. However, if you do have a frozen bird, it is most important to make sure that it is completely thawed before cooking. Wipe your turkey inside and out, and sprinkle it with sea salt.

The bird can be stuffed the night before, but the stuffing, if cooked at all, must be completely cold before use. The turkey must not be stuffed any earlier than the night before cooking. The stuffed bird should be smeared with 175 g/6 oz softened butter under the skin covering the breast as well as on top. You may also like to cover the breast with rashers of streaky bacon. Truss the turkey if you want a good shape, wrap the bird loosely in buttered cooking foil and place it in a roasting tin. Keep the turkey chilled until you are ready to cook it.

Roast the turkey for the time given in the chart below, basting it frequently during cooking. About 30 to 40 minutes before the end of the cooking time remove the foil so that the turkey will brown. Allow the cooked turkey to stand in a warm place, wrapped in a clean damp tea-towel, for 15 minutes before carving.

Mix a tablespoon of cornflour or arrowroot with a glass of white wine. Drain any excess grease from the juices left in the roasting tin and place the tin over a medium heat to bring the juices to the boil. Whisk in the wine mixture, and season to taste. Some people always strain the gravy for a smooth result, but I never do.

Most people have a favourite way of cooking turkey that they claim is the best. I'm always trying different methods; here are some of my notes. Whichever method you use, make sure the bird is the best and freshest you can buy.

Roasting Times for Turkey

Weigh the turkey and, following the times given below, roast the bird in a moderate oven (160 c, 325 f, gas 3).

2.5–3.5 kg/6–8 lb	$2\frac{3}{4}$–$3\frac{1}{4}$ hours	6–8 kg/14–18 lb	$4\frac{1}{4}$–$4\frac{3}{4}$ hours
3.5–4 kg/8–10 lb	$3\frac{1}{4}$–$3\frac{3}{4}$ hours	8–10 kg/18–20 lb	$4\frac{3}{4}$–$5\frac{1}{4}$ hours
4–6 kg/10–14 lb	$3\frac{3}{4}$–$4\frac{1}{4}$ hours		

Fruit Stuffing

1 cooking apple, washed and quartered
1 large orange, wiped and quartered
1 lemon, wiped and quartered
1 onion, peeled
100 g/4 oz chilled butter, diced

Put all the ingredients into the body cavity of the turkey, removing any pips from the fruit. At the end of the roasting time, transfer the turkey to a heated serving dish. Spoon the stuffing out of the bird and place it in a liquidiser or food processor. Process until smooth, then taste for seasoning. Keep the stuffing hot until the turkey is served.

Apricot, Rice and Nuts

2 onions, peeled and diced
25 g/1 oz butter
the turkey liver, diced
100 g/4 oz cooked brown rice (slightly undercooked is best)
salt and pepper
75 g/3 oz dried apricots, chopped
75 g/3 oz hazelnuts, halved and toasted
50 g/2 oz raisins
1 egg

Cook the onions in the butter until soft and golden. Add the turkey liver and continue to fry until browned. Stir in the rice, seasoning, apricots, nuts and raisins. Taste and adjust the seasoning if necessary, then stir in the egg. Allow the stuffing to cool, before carefully pressing it into the neck of the turkey (a small metal spoon is best for this).

Chestnut Stuffing

1 onion, peeled and chopped
25 g/1 oz butter
225 g/8 oz minced veal or pork sausagemeat
225 g/8 oz unsweetened chestnut purée
75 g/3 oz fresh brown breadcrumbs
1 tablespoon chopped celery
1 egg, beaten
salt and pepper

Cook the onion in the butter until soft. Cool, then mix with the other ingredients and stuff the mixture into the neck of the turkey.

Christmas Goose with Potato Stuffing

(Illustrated on page 28)

Goose is much more fatty than turkey, and does not go nearly as far.
Buy a 4.5-kg/10-lb dressed goose for 8 people.

1 young 4.5-kg/10-lb goose
1 tablespoon sea salt
75 g/3 oz butter, softened
2 large onions, finely chopped
450 g/1 lb potatoes
1 large cooking apple, peeled, cored and sliced
6 rindless rashers streaky bacon, diced
3 tablespoons double cream
salt and pepper
150 ml/$\frac{1}{4}$ pint port
600 ml/1 pint good poultry stock
a little arrowroot or cornflour (optional)

Wipe the goose inside and out, and rub both the cavity and skin with the salt. Smear 25 g/1 oz of the butter over the breast.

Cook the onions very slowly in the remaining butter until tender – about 20 minutes. Meanwhile, boil the potatoes for 10 minutes, then add the apple. Continue cooking for another 5 to 10 minutes, or until both the potatoes and apple are tender. Drain thoroughly and mash together until smooth. Dry-fry the bacon until crisp, then beat it into the potatoes with the cream and onions. Season to taste. Unless you are roasting the goose immediately, allow the stuffing to cool before filling the bird. Stuff the goose from the neck end and sew it up, then stand the bird in a roasting tin. Cover loosely with cooking foil and roast in a moderately hot oven (200 c, 400 f, gas 6) for 2$\frac{1}{2}$ hours, basting frequently.

Remove the foil, tip off the fat and pour the port over the goose. Return to the oven and cook, uncovered, for a further 10 to 15 minutes to crisp the skin. Transfer the goose to a heated serving dish and keep it hot. Pour the stock into the roasting tin and bring the liquid to the boil over a low heat, stirring continuously to remove any meat juices in the tin. If wished, thicken the sauce with a little cornflour or arrowroot blended with 1 or 2 tablespoons of cold water. Strain and pour into a gravy boat. **Serves 8**

Chicken with Avocado and Grapes

1 Iceberg lettuce or small Chinese cabbage, shredded *or* 1
bunch watercress, trimmed and shredded
675 g/1½ lb cold cooked chicken, cut into strips
225 g/8 oz seedless grapes
1 ripe avocado pear, sliced
75 g/3 oz blanched almonds, toasted until golden
150 ml/¼ pint soured cream
150 ml/¼ pint mayonnaise
salt and pepper

Arrange the lettuce, Chinese cabbage or watercress on a large serving
plate. Mix the chicken, grapes, sliced avocado and almonds in a bowl.
Combine the soured cream, mayonnaise and seasoning to taste, then
pour this dressing over the chicken. Fold together gently, pile on top of
the lettuce and chill until ready to serve. **Serves 6**

Chicken and Peach Salad

(Illustrated on pages 66/67)

2 (411-g/14½-oz) cans white peaches, drained
(you can also use ordinary peaches)
300 ml/½ pint mayonnaise
675 g/1½ lb cooked chicken
1 bunch spring onions, thinly sliced lengthways
¼ teaspoon dried tarragon
2 teaspoons lemon juice · salt and pepper
1 lettuce · sprigs of parsley to garnish

Purée two peaches from one can in a liquidiser and blend until smooth,
then stir this peach purée into the mayonnaise.

Cut the chicken into strips. Slice the remaining peaches, reserve a few
slices for garnish and mix the rest with the chicken and spring onions.
Fold into the mayonnaise mixture with the tarragon and lemon juice.
Season to taste and mix well.

Wash and dry the lettuce. Arrange the leaves on a serving dish and
pile the chicken mixture on top, leaving a border of lettuce showing.
Arrange the reserved peaches around the chicken mixture. Garnish with
sprigs of parsley and serve very cold. **Serves 6**

Tipsy Chicken

(Illustrated on page 45)

2 tablespoons oil
25 g/1 oz butter
1 (1.5-kg/3-lb) chicken
2 medium onions, thinly sliced
450 g/1 lb cooking apples, peeled, cored and sliced
175 g/6 oz prunes, stoned (use those which do not require
pre-soaking)
6 tablespoons calvados
4 teaspoons flour
600 ml/1 pint chicken stock
salt and pepper · 2 bay leaves
4 tablespoons soured cream
GARNISH
450 g/1 lb cooking apples
25 g/1 oz caster sugar
40 g/1½ oz butter

Heat the oil and butter together in a heavy-based flameproof casserole and thoroughly brown the chicken on all sides. Remove the chicken, then lower the heat, add the onions and cook slowly until soft but not brown – about 10 minutes. Add the sliced apples, and stir-fry over a moderate heat until both the apples and the onions are golden brown. Replace the chicken and add the prunes and the calvados, then immediately set the calvados alight. When the flames have died, stir the flour into the juices round the edge of the casserole. Pour in the stock, add seasoning and bay leaves and bring to the boil. Cover and cook in a moderate oven (180 c, 350 f, gas 4) for 50 minutes or until the chicken is cooked through and tender.

Meanwhile, prepare the garnish. Wash the unpeeled apples, then thickly slice them and neatly remove the cores. Dip the slices in sugar and fry them in the butter (use a non-stick frying pan if possible) until caramelised – about 4 minutes on each side. Keep hot.

Remove the cooked chicken from the casserole and divide it into six portions, or serve it whole if you like; keep the bird hot. Remove the prunes from the sauce and keep them hot too. Blend the sauce in a liquidiser until smooth – the apples and onions will help to thicken it – then pour it back into the casserole and boil until the sauce is of a coating consistency. Add the soured cream, taste and adjust the seasoning.

Arrange the chicken on a serving dish and garnish with the apple rings and prunes. Spoon a little sauce over the top and serve the rest separately. **Serves 6**

Christmas Duck

1 (2.5-kg/5$\frac{1}{2}$-lb) fresh duck
1 teaspoon sea salt
1 orange, pricked all over
3 tablespoons coarse bitter marmalade
2 tablespoons soy sauce
1 small carrot, diced
1 onion, chopped
1 tablespoon flour
2 tablespoons frozen concentrated orange juice
1$\frac{1}{2}$ tablespoons lemon juice
300 ml/$\frac{1}{2}$ pint poultry stock
1 tablespoon sherry or orange liqueur
pepper

Wipe the duck, inside and out, with a damp cloth. Prick it all over with a fork, then rub the salt all over it, both inside and out. Place the orange inside the duck and leave to stand for 1 hour in a cool place. Stand the duck on a rack in a roasting tin and cook in a moderately hot oven (200 c, 400 f, gas 6) for 1$\frac{1}{2}$ hours, turning the bird every 30 minutes. Start the cooking process with the breast side up, then turn the bird so that it sits on one side, then finally turn it so that it rests on the other side.

Remove the duck from the oven, pour off the fat from the roasting tin leaving the juices in the bottom of the pan. Mix the marmalade and soy sauce and paint half this mixture all over the duck. Put the carrot, onion and liver from the duck into the roasting tin and return it to the oven. Cook for a further 15 to 20 minutes, or until the skin is crisp and browned. Remove the duck, pouring the juices from the body cavity into the tin. Place the bird on a serving dish and keep hot.

Sprinkle the flour into the roasting tin and cook over a low heat, stirring, until lightly browned. Add the orange juice, lemon juice and stock and bring to the boil, stirring constantly. Simmer for a couple of minutes, then strain this sauce into a small saucepan and add the remaining marmalade mixture, sherry or orange liqueur and pepper to taste. Bring to the boil and tip any juices from the duck into the pan. Serve immediately, with the duck. **Serves 4**

Game Pie

A pie is ideal for using up cooked game. This recipe can be made from any game — pheasant, woodcock, grouse, wild duck, pigeon or a mixture. Alternatively, use chicken or turkey.

ROUGH PUFF PASTRY
275 g/10 oz plain flour
generous pinch of salt
175 g/6 oz butter, chilled and cut into dice
25 g/1 oz lard or white cooking fat,
chilled and cut into dice
175 ml/6 fl oz ice-cold water
1 teaspoon lemon juice

FILLING
450 g/1 lb cooked game,
free from skin and bone
25 g/1 oz butter
1 small onion, chopped
225 g/8 oz button mushrooms, sliced
2 tablespoons chopped parsley
1 tablespoon flour
175 ml/6 fl oz leftover gravy
or well-flavoured stock
salt and pepper
2 hard-boiled eggs
4 rindless rashers streaky bacon, halved
1 (90-g/3½-oz) can pâté de foie gras (optional)
1 egg, beaten

I don't like game and never eat it, but I have included this recipe for those of you who like game at this time of year.

To make the pastry, sift the flour into a bowl with the salt. Add the fats and, stirring quickly, use a palette knife to coat the pieces of fat in flour. Mix the water and lemon juice and stir this liquid into the flour mixture to make a soft, not sticky, dough with visible lumps of fat. Turn the dough out on to a floured surface and shape it into a rectangle. Roll out into a rectangle measuring about 33×11 cm/$13 \times 4\frac{1}{2}$ in, fold the lower third over the middle, then fold the top third down over the first fold. Press the edges together lightly and turn the pastry so that the folded edge is on your left. Re-roll the pastry into a rectangle which is slightly larger than the original one and repeat the folding process. Turn the pastry again and repeat this rolling and folding process four times. Wrap and chill the pastry while you prepare the filling.

Cut the game into bite-sized pieces. Melt the butter in a heavy-based saucepan and cook the onion over a gentle heat with the lid on the saucepan. Stir occasionally, then, after 10 minutes, increase the heat and add the mushrooms. Fry quickly before adding the parsley and flour, followed by the gravy or stock. Stir continuously to prevent lumps from forming. Cook over a medium heat until the sauce boils, then add seasoning to taste and stir in the meat. Transfer to a deep pie dish.

Quarter the eggs and wrap each quarter in a piece of bacon. Arrange these on top of the meat. Cut the pâté (if used) into fingers and put them between the eggs.

Roll out the pastry into a sheet large enough to cover the pie with 5 cm/2 in to spare. Cut a 1-cm/$\frac{1}{2}$-in strip from round the edge of the pastry and press this around the edge of the dish. Brush the pastry rim with beaten egg and lift the pastry lid over the pie. Seal and flute the edges, then cut a small hole in the top of the pie to allow the steam to escape. Use any pastry trimmings to decorate the top of the pie. Glaze with beaten egg and bake in a hot oven (220 C, 425 F, gas 7) for 30 minutes. Reduce the temperature to moderately hot (190 C. 375 F, gas 5) and cook for a further 10 minutes. Serve hot or cold **Serves 6**

Grilled Poussins with Honey and Lemon

4 (450-g/1-lb) poussins
1$\frac{1}{2}$ teaspoons sea salt
4 tablespoons lemon juice
4 tablespoons melted butter
4 tablespoons clear honey
4 almonds, cut into slivers

Use poultry scissors to snip on either side of the backbones in the poussins. Cut out the backbones completely, then turn the birds over and flatten them. Cut off the wing tips and wipe the poussins with a damp cloth. Thread the birds on to skewers to keep them open and flat, then rub them all over with salt and sprinkle with lemon juice. Leave to marinate for 15 minutes.

Brush the poussins with the melted butter and cook them under a hot grill for 25 minutes, turning and basting them frequently. Brush with honey and grill for a further 5 minutes, again basting and turning them all the time. Sprinkle with the almonds and continue to grill until golden, then serve very hot, garnished with lemon wedges, with rice as an accompaniment. Alternatively, serve the poussins cold with a salad.
Serves 4

Festive Pheasant

Pheasants are usually plentiful around Christmas time, and cooking them this way not only makes them moist and tender but it is also a change from making a rich sauce. Chicken can be used instead of pheasant if you like.

2 pheasants · 75 g/3 oz butter
1 (425-g/15-oz) can pineapple cubes in natural juice
150 ml/¼ pint well-flavoured game stock
225 g/8 oz seedless grapes · salt and pepper
3 teaspoons arrowroot mixed with a little water
lemon juice to taste
1 orange, peeled and cut into segments

Wipe the pheasants inside and out with a damp cloth and truss them neatly. Melt the butter in a heavy flameproof casserole, then brown the pheasants, one at a time, on all sides. Place both pheasants in the casserole and add the pineapple cubes with their juice, the stock and the grapes. Season with salt and pepper. Cover and cook in a moderate oven (180 C, 350 F, gas 4) for 1 to 1½ hours or until tender. Transfer the pheasants to a heated serving dish, remove any string and keep hot.

Strain the sauce, reserving the fruit. Bring the liquid to the boil and stir in the arrowroot mixture. Add the lemon juice and adjust the seasoning. Stir in the reserved fruit and orange segments. Pour a little sauce over the birds; hand the rest separately. **Serves 4 to 6**

Veal in Stilton Sauce

6 thin escalopes of veal, pork or turkey
75 g/3 oz butter · 300 ml/½ pint soured cream
100 g/4 oz ripe Stilton cheese, crumbled
black pepper to taste

Trim the meat. Heat the butter in a large heavy-based frying pan. Add the escalopes and fry for 1 to 2 minutes on each side, or until they are golden brown. Remove the meat from the pan, transfer to a heated serving dish and keep hot.

Add the cream to the fat remaining in the pan and stir well over a low heat to dissolve any meat juices. Stir in the Stilton and season with black pepper, then pour this over the meat and serve with a salad. **Serves 6**

Beef Loaf

1 kg/2 lb chuck steak, minced
4 tablespoons fresh breadcrumbs
$\frac{1}{2}$ red pepper, deseeded and finely chopped
1 large onion, grated
1 tablespoon tomato purée
$\frac{1}{2}$ teaspoon dried mixed herbs
salt and pepper
2 eggs, lightly beaten
FILLING
350 g/12 oz mashed potato
100 g/4 oz Cheddar cheese, grated
salt and pepper
TOPPING
75 g/3 oz cheese, sliced (optional)
Home-made Tomato Sauce (page 63)

Good for those meals when you have a mixture of children and adults. This beef roll is also delicious cold with chutney. Alternative fillings: chopped spinach and cottage cheese, or mashed cooked carrots.

In a large mixing bowl, combine the minced steak, breadcrumbs, chopped red pepper, onion, tomato purée, herbs and seasoning; mix well. Add the lightly beaten eggs and stir well until the mixture is thoroughly combined. For the filling, combine the mashed potato, grated cheese and seasoning until smooth.

Lay a sheet of greaseproof paper flat on a work surface and turn the meat mixture out on to it. Shape the meat into a flat rectangle of even thickness (about 1.5 cm/$\frac{3}{4}$ in thick) and about 23 × 33 cm/9 × 13 in. in size. Make sure the meat is thoroughly bound together. Pile the potato mixture down the middle of the meat, then carefully lift one edge of the greaseproof paper and fold the meat over the potato filling (it should come about halfway over the top). Now lift the opposite side and fold the meat over to completely enclose the potato. The greaseproof paper should lift off the meat quite easily: it should not stick. Roll the paper back slightly and pinch the join in the meat together quite securely. Pinch the meat at the ends of the roll to completely enclose the filling. Use the greaseproof paper to lift the meat on to a large baking tray or roasting tin, then carefully roll the loaf off the paper (on to the tin) so that the join in the meat is underneath. Check that the ends are well sealed: if the meat does not completely enclose the filling the potato will run out during cooking.

Bake in a moderate oven (160 c, 325 f, gas 3) for 1$\frac{1}{2}$ hours. Overlap the slices of cheese (if used) on top of the meat and bake for a further 15 minutes or until the cheese melts. Serve hot or cold, cut into slices. If serving hot, carefully lift the roll on to a serving dish and pour the Home-made Tomato Sauce over the top. **Serves 6**

Beef Casserole with Walnuts

1 kg/2 lb lean chuck steak
600 ml/1 pint Guinness
4 large onions, thinly sliced
50 g/2 oz root ginger, peeled and chopped
4 tablespoons oil
1 bay leaf
1 teaspooon mixed spice
1 tablespoon flour
salt and pepper
75–100 g/3–4 oz walnut halves

Cut the beef into large cubes and put them in a china, glass or earthenware bowl with the Guinness, sliced onions, finely chopped ginger, 1 tablespoon of the oil, the bay leaf and mixed spice. Mix well, then cover and leave to marinate in a cool place for 1 to 2 hours.

When ready to cook the casserole, remove the cubes of beef from the marinade and pat them dry on absorbent kitchen paper. Heat the remaining oil in a heavy flameproof casserole. Add the beef and brown thoroughly on all sides – you'll probably find that it is best to do this in several batches. Remove and set aside.

Strain the marinade, reserving the liquid and the vegetables. Add the onions, and ginger to the oil in the casserole, and cook over low heat, stirring frequently, until soft and transparent. Stir in the flour, followed by the liquid from the marinade. Bring to the boil, stirring constantly, then add the bay leaf, the meat and its juices, salt and pepper and the walnuts. Stir gently, then cover and cook in a moderate oven (180 C, 350 F, gas 4) for 45 minutes. Stir gently, replace the cover and reduce the heat to (160 C, 325 F, gas 3). Cook for a further 45 minutes or until the meat is very tender. Stir gently and taste for seasoning before serving with Red Cabbage with Apples and Prunes (page 52) and Creamed Potatoes with Celeriac (page 50). **Serves 6 to 8**

Beef Bourguignonne

1 kg/2 lb lean chuck steak, cut into cubes
50 g/2 oz plain flour · 3 tablespoons oil
2 large onions, chopped
2 carrots, thinly sliced
2 cloves garlic, crushed · ½ bottle red wine
bouquet garni
1 tablespoon chopped parsley
salt and pepper

I sometimes cut out shapes of puff pastry and bake them until golden, then arrange them on the beef just before serving.

Toss the meat in the flour until well covered. Heat the oil until very hot, then sauté the meat a few pieces at a time until brown. Transfer the pieces to an ovenproof casserole dish.

Fry the onions, carrots and garlic in the remaining fat. Add the wine, bouquet garni, parsley and seasoning. Stir well and pour over the meat. Cook in a moderate oven (160 c, 325 f, gas 3) for 3 hours. **Serves 6**

Lamb Stuffed with Fruit

1 (2.5-kg/5-lb) leg of lamb, boned and flattened
pinch of sea salt
225 g/8 oz dried mixed fruit
50 g/2 oz butter · 1 tablespoon chopped onion
2 sticks celery, finely chopped
25 g/1 oz fresh breadcrumbs
1 tablespoon juniper berries, crushed
2 tablespoons redcurrant jelly

With this I serve drained pear halves with a spoonful of redcurrant or mint jelly in each half.

Sprinkle the lamb with coarse salt. Set aside 4 tablespoons of the mixed fruit. Melt the butter in a frying pan and sauté the onion and celery in it until soft, but not brown. Add the breadcrumbs and fruit and stir together until mixed. Spoon this filling over the flattened lamb, leaving a 1-cm/½-in border all round. Roll up, starting from the long side, and tie neatly in shape with string. Place the joint in a roasting tin, seam-side down and sprinkle the juniper berries on top.

Roast the lamb in a moderate oven (180 c, 350 f, gas 4) for 2 to 2½ hours. About 30 minutes before the end of the cooking time spread the redcurrant jelly over the meat. Make a gravy in the usual way, using the cooking juices, vegetable water and thickening if you like. Add the reserved fruit to the gravy. **Serves 8**

Glazed Ham with Orange Sauce

(Illustrated on pages 66/67)

joint of middle or corner gammon (about 1.8 kg/4 lb in
weight)
1 large onion
1 bay leaf
6 peppercorns
75 g/3 oz soft brown sugar
1 teaspoon dry mustard
cloves
ORANGE SAUCE
2 tablespoons redcurrant or quince jelly
grated rind and juice of 3 oranges
grated rind and juice of 1 lemon
2 teaspoons creamed horseradish
1 teaspoon French mustard
1 teaspoon vinegar

Soak the gammon overnight in cold water. Drain the meat and put it in
a large saucepan with cold water to cover, the onion, bay leaf and
peppercorns. Bring to the boil, skim the surface of the water and reduce
the heat. Cover, then simmer for $1\frac{1}{2}$ hours.

Remove the joint from the pan, peel off the skin and mark the fat into
diamond shapes with a sharp knife. Reserve the stock, if you like, for
making soup. Stand the gammon in a roasting tin. Mix the sugar and
mustard together and press this over the fat. Press a clove into the corner
of each diamond. Roast in a hot oven (220 C, 425 F, gas 7) for about 15 to
30 minutes or until the fat is crisp and golden.

Meanwhile, make the orange sauce. Melt the redcurrant or quince
jelly in a saucepan, add the fruit rind and juice and stir well. Stir in the
horseradish, mustard and vinegar and heat through. This sweet and sour
sauce can be served either hot or cold. **Serves 8**

Opposite page Tipsy Chicken (page 36) and Vegetable
Terrine (page 54)
Overleaf The Christmas Meal: Christmas Turkey (page 32) with
Beetroot Mashed Potatoes (page 53) and steamed broccoli; Cloutie
Dumpling (page 92)

Side Effects

Because I always like recipes to be adaptable, some of the following ideas are suitable for serving on their own as a lunch or supper dish as well as being an accompaniment to your main course. I still think that fresh vegetables, steamed with a sprinkling of herbs, lemon juice or a knob of butter, are unbeatable. And at this time of year there are still many vegetables available to choose from.

Here are some ideas: mangetout peas can be steamed for only one minute or used raw in a salad; Brussels sprouts are delicious served with fried breadcrumbs and walnuts instead of the usual chestnuts, and potatoes can be mashed with finely chopped spring onions or served with a spoonful of cream on top and lots of chopped chives, or pine nuts. Try serving a purée of carrots sprinkled with nutmeg, or steamed celery sprinkled with caraway seeds.

If your main course is rich, serve a very simple vegetable or green salad. With leftover cold meats for instance, go to town on the side effects.

Opposite page Watercress and Orange Salad with Walnuts (page 59)
and Artist's Salad (page 58)

Vegetable Ideas

I think the nicest way to cook vegetables is to steam them with a
squeeze of lemon juice. But here are some suggestions.

Creamed Potatoes with Celeriac Cook together, in salted
simmering water, an equal quantity of potatoes and celeriac (peeled and
cut into even-sized pieces). When the vegetables are tender, drain and
mash them together until smooth. Beat in a little hot milk and a large
knob of butter with salt and pepper to taste. Add a little freshly grated
nutmeg and serve immediately.

Celeriac Purée Cook the celeriac, peeled and cut into even-sized
pieces, in salted simmering water until tender. Drain and mash
thoroughly, then beat in a little butter and cream (or top of the milk).
Add seasoning to taste and some chopped fresh chives or parsley.

Carrot Purée Purée cooked carrots in a food processor or by passing
the mashed vegetables through a fine sieve. Add a knob of butter and a
spoonful of cream.

Spinach and Pear Purée Peel, core and dice two ripe pears. Put them
in a saucepan with a large knob of butter and cook gently for a few
minutes. Add 450 g/1 lb frozen leaf spinach and cook gently until
thawed. Boil rapidly until the excess liquid has evaporated, then purée
the mixture in a liquidiser or food processor. Season with salt, pepper
and a little grated nutmeg, add a knob of butter and serve.

Roast Parsnips Peel and quarter as many parsnips as you need. Blanch
the vegetables in boiling salted water for 1 minute, then drain them and
dust the pieces with a little flour. Roast the parsnips with a joint or bird,
in a roasting tin, adding a little oil or lard if necessary. The vegetables
should take about 1 hour to cook (depending on the oven temperature).
Turn and baste the parsnips occasionally; when cooked they should be
brown and crisp.

Braised Vegetables These can be cooked in the oven at the same time
as the meat. To braise chicory or leeks, trim and blanch the vegetables in
boiling salted water for 1 minute. Melt 40 g/1½ oz butter in a flameproof
casserole, then add a couple of sliced onions, a chopped carrot and a
sliced stick of celery. Cook gently for about 15 minutes, then add a little
fresh thyme, a few sprigs of parsley and a bay leaf. Pour in enough stock
or water to just cover the vegetables and add seasoning to taste. Lay the
leeks or celery on top and cover the casserole, then cook in a moderate

oven (180 c, 350 f, gas 4) for about 30 to 40 minutes, or until tender. Transfer the cooked vegetables to a heated serving dish. Strain and thicken the cooking liquid if you like, then pour it over the vegetables. Serve immediately.

Steamed Vegetables Vegetables can be steamed over a pan of boiling soup, ham or even a pudding. Prepare the vegetables as for boiling, season them with a little salt and serve with butter.

Ratatouille

3 aubergines
salt and pepper
6 tablespoons olive oil
2 large onions, chopped
4 tomatoes, peeled, deseeded and roughly chopped
6 medium courgettes, cut into strips
1 large red pepper, deseeded and cut into strips
1 large green pepper, deseeded and cut into strips
1 large yellow pepper, deseeded and cut into strips
ground coriander to taste
3 cloves garlic, crushed
a couple of sprigs of fresh thyme
3 tablespoons chopped parsley

Wipe the aubergines, trim off their stalks and cut them into fingers. Place in a colander, sprinkle with salt and set aside for 30 minutes. Rinse the soaked aubergines in cold water, then drain and pat them dry with absorbent kitchen paper.

Heat a little of the oil in a frying pan. Add the aubergines and fry briefly over high heat until golden brown. Remove and drain on absorbent kitchen paper. Add a little more oil and fry all the remaining vegetables individually in the same way. Keep the vegetables separate; season each with a little salt, pepper and coriander. Layer the vegetables with the garlic in an ovenproof casserole, sprinkling in the thyme. Cover and bake in a moderately hot oven (190 c, 375 f, gas 5) for 30 to 35 minutes or until tender. Sprinkle with the parsley before serving either hot or cold. **Serves 6**

Make a lot – it's useful at Christmas. Have it hot or cold, or as a supper dish with sliced mozzarella cheese melted on top.

Carrot Pudding

675 g/1½ lb carrots, peeled and sliced
900 ml/1½ pints chicken stock
1 teaspoon sugar
2 teaspoons oil
knob of butter
1 onion, finely chopped
4 eggs, lightly beaten
225 g/8 oz Cheddar or Gruyère cheese, grated
50 g/2 oz fresh breadcrumbs
2 teaspoons chopped chives or parsley

Served with herb bread, this is nice as a first course.

Cook the carrots in the chicken stock until tender, then set aside to cool. When cool add the sugar and purée the mixture in a liquidiser.

In another saucepan, heat the oil and butter, then add the onion and cook gently until soft. Stir the cooked onion into the carrot purée with the lightly beaten eggs. Fold in 175 g/6 oz of the cheese and season to taste. Pour the carrot mixture into a lightly buttered shallow ovenproof dish. Sprinkle with the rest of the cheese, breadcrumbs and herbs.

Cook in a moderate oven (180 c, 350 F, gas 4) for 50 to 60 minutes or until the pudding is set. Serve immediately. **Serves 4 to 6**

Red Cabbage with Apples and Prunes

1 small red cabbage
large handful of prunes, stoned
2 apples, peeled and chopped
scant tablespoon brown sugar
175 ml/6 fl oz cider vinegar

Remove the hard central core, then chop or shred the red cabbage and put it into a large saucepan with the rest of the ingredients. Cook, covered, over a low heat, stirring from time to time, until the cabbage is tender – about 40 minutes. **Serves 4 to 6**

Note: This dish reheats very well.

Beetroot Mashed Potatoes

(Illustrated on pages 46/47)

1 kg/2 lb potatoes
4 tablespoons milk
50 g/2 oz butter
salt and pepper
100 g/4 oz uncooked beetroot

This may sound odd but the taste is lovely and so is the colour; it cheers up bangers and mash.

Peel the potatoes and cut them into even-sized pieces. Cook them in simmering salted water until tender, then mash the drained potatoes with the milk, butter, salt and pepper. Set aside and keep hot.

Wash, peel and grate the beetroot and add it to the mashed potato. Stir thoroughly until the potatoes have absorbed all the colour and the beetroot is evenly distributed. Serve immediately. This is excellent with plain roast meat, cold cooked chicken or turkey. **Serves 6 to 8**

Alternative ideas for mashed potato: mix grated raw carrrot, or toasted flaked almonds, or chopped spring onions into the potatoes before serving.

Yams in Orange Shells

(Illustrated on page 28)

Try this American idea – sweet potatoes or yams in orange shells. Topped with marshmallows, these can be prepared in advance, then heated in the oven until the marshmallow is browned.

1 kg/2 lb yams or sweet potatoes
2 tablespoons single cream
50 g/2 oz butter · salt and pepper
6 scooped-out oranges
a few small white marshmallows (optional)

When making fresh orange juice, put the orange shells in the freezer for later use in this sort of recipe.

Scrub and bake the yams or sweet potatoes in the oven until soft. Scoop the vegetables out of the shells and mash with the cream and butter, salt and pepper. Spoon this mixture into the orange shells, and serve right away as they are, or stand them in an ovenproof dish and top with marshmallows, then bake in a moderate oven (180 C, 350 F, gas 4) for 10 to 15 minutes or until the marshmallow begins to brown. **Serves 6**

Vegetable Terrine

(Illustrated on page 45)

This dish sounds complicated, but it's well worth the extra effort.

CARROT MIXTURE
225 g/8 oz carrots, peeled and cut into small pieces
2 egg yolks
2 tablespoons double cream · salt and pepper
SPINACH MIXTURE
450 g/1 lb frozen chopped spinach, thawed
2 tablespoons double cream
2 egg yolks
salt and pepper · pinch of nutmeg
15 g/½ oz flour
CAULIFLOWER MIXTURE
225 g/8 oz cauliflower, cut into small pieces
2 tablespoons double cream
2 egg yolks · salt and pepper
3 egg whites (divided between all the above mixtures)
HOLLANDAISE SAUCE
2 tablespoons white wine vinegar
3 tablespoons lemon juice
6 egg yolks · salt and pepper
350 g/12 oz unsalted butter, melted
2 tablespoons chopped fresh herbs
1 tomato, peeled, deseeded and diced

I save time by using my food processor for this.

First, prepare the carrot mixture: purée the uncooked carrots in a food processor. Then blend with the egg yolks and cream, adding seasoning to taste. For the spinach mixture, you must first squeeze all the liquid from the chopped spinach. Purée the spinach with the cream, egg yolks, seasoning, nutmeg and flour. Finally, purée the uncooked cauliflower, then blend in the cream, egg yolks and seasoning.

Whisk the egg whites until they stand in stiff peaks, then divide them equally between the three mixtures and fold in gently using a metal spoon. Line and grease a 1-kg/2-lb loaf tin. Spread the spinach mixture in the base of the tin and smooth over the top to give an even layer. Next spoon the cauliflower mixture on top and smooth the top. Lastly top with the carrot mixture. Cover with greased cooking foil and stand the tin in a roasting tin half filled with hot water. Bake in a moderate oven (160 c, 325 f, gas 3) for 2½ hours, or until set. Cool slightly in the tin before turning out on to a heated serving dish.

Towards the end of the cooking time make the sauce: bring the vinegar and lemon juice to the boil. Put the egg yolks in a liquidiser or food processor with a little seasoning. Blend briefly, then gradually pour in the hot vinegar mixture followed by the melted butter. Do not pour the butter in too quickly or the sauce will curdle. Transfer the sauce to a warmed sauce boat or dish, stir in the herbs and diced tomato, and adjust the seasoning if necessary. Serve the sauce to accompany the terrine. **Serves 8 to 10**

Vegetable Pie

This is particularly useful for a vegetarian meal. Try different combinations of vegetables — you can't go wrong!

2 large onions, sliced
1 tablespoon oil
4 carrots, sliced
3 courgettes, sliced
1 cauliflower, divided into florets
salt and pepper
75 g/3 oz plain flour
75 g/3 oz butter
900 ml/1½ pints milk
1 tablespoon chopped fresh herbs (choose your favourite herbs
or tarragon is delicious)
100 g/4 oz cooked butter beans
1 (215-g/7½-oz) packet frozen puff pastry, thawed
beaten egg to glaze

Let yourself be carried away with the pastry decorations for this pie – flowers, leaves, hearts, initials or a guest's name – it's easy.

Sauté the onions in the oil until just soft. Drain on absorbent kitchen paper and set aside. Cook the prepared vegetables separately in salted simmering water for 10 minutes, or until tender but still crisp.

Meanwhile make the sauce: combine the flour, butter and milk together in a saucepan. Bring to the boil, whisking continuously, season, add the herbs and remove from the heat.

Drain the vegetables and arrange them (with the onions) in layers in a pie dish with the butter beans. Pour the sauce over the vegetables. Roll the pastry out into a piece large enough to cover the pie with 5 cm/2 in to spare. Cut a narrow strip from round the pastry and press this on the rim of the dish; brush with beaten egg. Lift the lid over the pie, seal and flute the edges, then glaze the top. Bake in a moderately hot oven (190 c, 375 f, gas 5) for 30 minutes. Serve hot. **Serves 6**

Pasta Salad

225 g/8 oz pasta shells, shapes or twists
150 ml/¼ pint mayonnaise
2 or 3 sticks celery, chopped
50 g/2 oz walnut pieces
black pepper
¼ teaspoon dried mixed herbs (or to taste)
lettuce leaves to serve

Louisa Moore (Roger's wife) makes a great pasta salad simply by mixing the cold cooked pasta with strips of pimiento, a vinaigrette dressing and plenty of freshly ground black pepper.

Cook the pasta in plenty of simmering salted water for 10 to 12 minutes or until just tender, drain and cool.

Put the pasta into a serving dish, pour over the mayonnaise and mix well until the pasta is evenly coated. Add the celery and walnuts and again mix well. Finally, season with black pepper and mixed herbs.

Cover and chill until required, and serve in a bowl lined with lettuce leaves. **Serves 4 to 6**

Brown Rice Salad

1.15 litres/2 pints water
1 teaspoon salt · 350 g/12 oz brown rice
2 large carrots, grated
12 spring onions, chopped
2 tablespoons chopped chives
2 tablespoons chopped parsley
100 g/4 oz white cabbage, grated
½ cucumber, chopped
6 tablespoons salad dressing of your choice
1 lettuce heart, broken into leaves
GARNISH
sprigs of watercress · tomato wedges

Bring the water and salt to the boil. Add the rice and cook for 30 to 40 minutes or until the grains are just tender, then drain thoroughly.

While the rice is still warm, mix in the grated carrots, spring onions, chives, parsley, cabbage and cucumber. Pour the salad dressing over and toss well. Press into a 1.15–litre/2–pint ring mould or pudding basin and leave to cool.

Arrange the lettuce heart on a serving platter. Invert the ring mould or basin on to the platter and lift the container off to serve the rice. Garnish before serving. **Serves 6**

Gazpacho Mould

15 g/½ oz gelatine · 250 ml/8 fl oz boiling water
1 chicken stock cube · 300 ml/½ pint tomato juice
1 tablespoon lemon juice · 2 teaspoons wine vinegar
½ teaspoon Worcestershire sauce
¼ teaspoon basil · 2 cloves garlic, crushed
2 tomatoes, peeled, deseeded and chopped
2 sticks celery, finely diced
¼ cucumber, peeled and chopped
½ green pepper, deseeded and finely chopped
1 tablespoon finely chopped spring onion
salad ingredients to garnish

Dissolve the gelatine in the boiling water, add and dissolve the stock cube. Stir in the next five ingredients and chill until half set.

Stir the remaining ingredients through the half-set mixture and season to taste, then pour into a rinsed-out 1.15-litre/2-pint mould and chill until set. To turn out, dip the bottom of the mould in hot water and place a serving platter over the top. Invert and lift the mould off the mixture to serve. Garnish with salad ingredients. **Serves 6**

Caesar Salad

(Illustrated on page 25)

1 clove garlic, finely chopped
200 ml/8 fl oz olive oil
100 g/4 oz white bread, cubed
75 g/3 oz butter · 2 eggs
2 cos lettuce, washed and torn into pieces
salt and pepper
juice of 1 lemon · 6–8 anchovy fillets
100 g/4 oz fresh Parmesan cheese, grated

Mix the garlic with 100 ml/4 fl oz of the olive oil a few hours before you are going to serve the salad. Sauté the cubes of bread in the butter until brown and crunchy, drain these croûtons and put aside.

Boil the eggs for exactly 1 minute. Cool. Strain the olive oil and mix it with the remaining unflavoured oil. Put the lettuce in a bowl, add seasoning and the oil and toss well. Break in the eggs, and the lemon juice, then toss again. Finally, add the anchovies, cheese and croûtons and toss carefully. Serve immediately. **Serves 8**

Artist's Salad

(Illustrated on page 48)

1 bunch watercress, finely chopped
1 bunch spring onions, shredded lengthways
2 large carrots, grated · 50 g/2 oz cheese, chopped
1 large uncooked beetroot, grated
2 large tomatoes, chopped
2 or 3 sticks celery, chopped
6 rindless rashers bacon, fried until crisp and crumbled
chopped parsley · florets of cauliflower
2 slices wholemeal bread, cut into squares and fried in butter
2 hard-boiled eggs, chopped
450 g/1 lb cooked chicken or turkey, cut into neat squares
1 Iceberg lettuce, cut into chunks
DRESSING
150 ml/$\frac{1}{4}$ pint soured cream
150 ml/$\frac{1}{4}$ pint mayonnaise

Use a large, shallow salad bowl or platter. Arrange the salad ingredients in separate piles, according to the best colour effect – like an artist's palette. Mix the dressing ingredients and serve it separately. Toss the ingredients in this only just before serving. Serve with French bread. **Serves 6**

Minted Carrot Salad

2 tablespoons vegetable oil
1 tablespoon lemon juice or orange juice
a few mint leaves, chopped · salt and pepper
450 g/1 lb large carrots, grated
sesame seeds, toasted · mint to garnish

Mix the oil with the lemon or orange juice, the chopped mint and a little salt and pepper. Toss the carrots in this mixture. Cover and chill for an hour for the flavours to blend. Toss again, sprinkle with sesame seeds and garnish with a few sprigs of mint. **Serves 4**

Note: For a stronger flavoured salad, replace the vegetable oil with olive oil,.and add a couple of crushed cloves of garlic with a little grated lemon or orange rind.

Watercress and Orange Salad with Walnuts

(Illustrated on page 48)

6 oranges
2 large bunches watercress, trimmed and rinsed
100 g/4 oz walnut pieces
DRESSING
the reserved juice from the oranges (see below)
4 tablespoons walnut or olive oil
1 tablespoon sherry or wine vinegar
$\frac{1}{4}$ teaspoon mustard powder
salt and pepper

Peel and slice the oranges into rounds, keeping the juice for the dressing, then cut these slices in half. Mix the watercress, oranges and walnuts.

Mix all the ingredients for the dressing and taste for seasoning; pour over the salad and toss well to mix. Serve immediately. **Serves 4 to 6**

Warm Spinach Salad

450 g/1 lb tender young spinach
6 spring onions, finely chopped
$\frac{1}{2}$ clove garlic
1 tablespoon salad oil
3 rindless rashers bacon
1 tablespoon sugar
1 tablespoon tarragon vinegar
1 tablespoon red wine vinegar
1 egg · salt and pepper

Wash and dry the spinach, tear it into small pieces and transfer to a salad bowl; add the spring onions. Mash the garlic into the oil and leave to stand, whilst preparing the rest of the salad. Dry-fry the bacon gently until very crisp, drain, crumble and add it to the spinach. Strain the garlic from the oil and pour the oil over the salad.

Whisk the sugar, vinegars, egg and seasoning together, pour into the bacon fat remaining in the pan and stir gently for a few seconds over a low heat until the egg mixture has thickened slightly.

Pour over the spinach and toss the salad so that all the ingredients are evenly combined. Serve immediately. **Serves 6**

Tomato and Mozzarella Salad

(Illustrated on pages 26/27)

6 large, ripe tomatoes
150 ml/¼ pint olive oil
2 tablespoons sherry or red wine vinegar
salt and pepper · ½ teaspoon mustard powder
2 teaspoons chopped basil (or other fresh herbs)
100 g/4 oz mozzarella cheese, thinly sliced
Garnish (optional)
50 g/2 oz black olives or stuffed green olives
sprigs of watercress
a few toasted whole hazelnuts

Using a very sharp knife, cut the tomatoes into thin slices. Arrange these in a salad bowl or individual dishes. Whisk together the olive oil, sherry or vinegar, seasoning and mustard to make a dressing. Stir in the basil or other herbs, taste and adjust the seasoning if necessary. Spoon the dressing over the tomatoes, cover and chill for an hour, or until ready to eat. Arrange the mozzarella on the tomatoes and garnish, if you like. Serve immediately, with hot garlic or herb bread. **Serves 4 to 6**

Pineapple, Pepper and Cottage Cheese Salad

(Illustrated on pages 26/27)

The combination of pineapple, nuts and cottage cheese, makes an excellent accompaniment to a simple grilled meat dish. This salad can even be served as a pudding, or as lunch for the weight watchers.

1 ripe pineapple · 225 g/8 oz cottage cheese
50 g/2 oz salted cashew nuts
2 sticks celery, finely chopped
1 green pepper, deseeded and finely chopped

Cut the pineapple in half lengthways. Cut out the flesh, remove the core and chop the fruit into chunks. Reserve the pineapple shell. Mix the pineapple chunks with the cottage cheese, cashew nuts, chopped celery and green pepper. Mix well and chill until required.

Spoon the salad into the reserved fruit shells and serve on a bed of lettuce, garnished, if you wish, with extra pepper slices. **Serves 4**

Dressing Up

Vinaigrette Dressing

Everyone has a favourite dressing; this is my basic standby to which I add various ingredients according to the type of salad.

Mix one-third vinegar to sunflower or safflower oil, add 1 teaspoon honey, $\frac{1}{2}$ teaspoon Dijon mustard, salt, pepper and 1 tablespoon finely chopped herbs. I make a fairly large quantity in a screw-topped jar and leave it in the refrigerator to save time.

Onion and Garlic Dressing

3 tablespoons finely chopped spring onion
1 clove garlic, crushed · 250 ml/8 fl oz mayonnaise
2 tablespoons cider or wine vinegar
4 tablespoons soured cream · 3 tablespoons lemon juice
1 tablespoon chopped parsley
salt and pepper · pinch of nutmeg

Mix all the ingredients together, then cover and chill until required.
Makes 450 ml/$\frac{3}{4}$ pint

Cream Cheese Dressing

75 g/3 oz cream cheese · 1 tablespoon lemon juice
2 tablespoons redcurrant jelly · 150 ml/$\frac{1}{4}$ pint double cream

Place all the ingredients in a bowl and mix together until smooth. Serve with either a savoury salad or with a fruit salad, or mince pies. **Makes about 250 ml/8 fl oz**

Butters for Hot French Bread

Herb Butter

Mash a few tablespoons of chopped fresh herbs – parsley, chives and chervil, for example – into softened butter. Shape into a roll, wrap in foil and chill until needed.

Anchovy Butter

Blend about 1 (50-g/1$\frac{3}{4}$-oz) can anchovies (or more or less to taste) for each 225 g/8 oz butter, then mix in the butter and shape as above.

Three Ways to Make Good Gravy

Gravy is usually made from the juices left in the roasting tin but it can also be made in a frying pan using the juices from frying a steak or chops, or even in a grill pan using the juices from grilled chicken or sausages.

Gravy can be thick or thin; it can be thickened with flour, cornflour, arrowroot, or beurre manié (a paste of butter and flour). Alternatively the juices can be seasoned and served unthickened.

Traditional Gravy To give a gravy from a roast lots of flavour, stand the joint or poultry on a bed of quartered onions and carrots in a roasting tin, with any bones from the meat. Baste the joint frequently during cooking, then when it is cooked remove it from the roasting tin and keep hot. Pour off any excess fat, leaving the meat juices, sediment and the vegetables. Over low heat, add a generous tablespoon of flour and stir well to dislodge all the sediment and absorb all the juices. The flour mixture should bubble and turn golden brown. Stir in 450 ml/$\frac{3}{4}$ pint good meat stock or vegetable cooking liquid, then bring to the boil stirring continuously. Simmer for 3 minutes, then season to taste with salt and pepper. Strain, if you like, and serve very hot.

For an unthickened gravy, follow the method above but omit the flour. Simmer the gravy for about 5 minutes until reduced and syrupy. Cornflour and arrowroot can also be used to thicken gravies. Mix a generous tablespoon of cornflour with 4 tablespoons cold water, stock or cold vegetable cooking liquid until smooth. Stir into 450 ml/$\frac{3}{4}$ pint boiling gravy and simmer for a minute. Alternatively, mix 3 teaspoons of arrowroot to a paste with a little water and add this to 450 ml/$\frac{3}{4}$ pint boiling gravy. Do not reheat or boil for more than a few seconds or the sauce will thin again.

To make a beurre manié blend 40 g/$1\frac{1}{2}$ oz softened butter into the same quantity of flour to make a smooth paste. Stir this vigorously into the boiling liquid and simmer for 3 minutes.

Extra Special Gravy Follow the method for traditional gravy but replace half the stock with a strong or full-bodied red wine or port. Allow to simmer 5 to 6 minutes before straining. This gravy is excellent with red meats and game.

Rich Onion Gravy Peel and thinly slice 6 medium onions. Melt 75 g/ 3 oz butter in a heavy-based saucepan, add the onions with a bay leaf and a little salt and pepper. Stir well, then cover with a piece of damp greaseproof paper and the saucepan lid. Cook very gently, stirring now and then, until very soft and golden – about 15 to 20 minutes. Blend 40 g/1½ oz of soft butter with an equal quantity of flour and stir into the mixture. Pour in 450 ml/¾ pint stock and bring to the boil. Stir in 1 tablespoon chopped parsley or chives just before serving.

Home-made Tomato Sauce

25 g/1 oz butter
1 large onion, finely chopped
2 carrots, finely chopped
1 (397-g/14-oz) can tomatoes
300 ml/½ pint tomato juice
2 tablespoons tomato purée
2 teaspoons sugar
3 teaspoons vinegar
1½ teaspoons Worcestershire sauce
¾ teaspoon dried mixed herbs
pinch of nutmeg
pinch of allspice
¼ teaspoon salt
black pepper

Melt the butter in a saucepan, add the onion and carrots, and sauté until the onions are soft but not brown. Drain the tomatoes and reserve the juice, chop the tomatoes and add them to the sautéed vegetables. Add the juice from the can with the 300 ml/½ pint tomato juice and purée and stir well. Bring to the boil, then turn down the heat so that the sauce simmers gently for 15 minutes.

Stir in the sugar, vinegar, Worcestershire sauce, herbs, spices and seasoning. When the carrots are tender transfer the sauce to a liquidiser and blend until smooth. **Makes 900 ml/1½ pints**

Note: Home-made tomato sauce can be kept in the refrigerator until ready for serving – for example with a quick spaghetti, a meatloaf or as a filling for an omelette.

Bread Sauce

3 cloves
1 small onion, peeled
1 bay leaf
a few sprigs of parsley
450 ml/$\frac{3}{4}$ pint milk
75 g/3 oz fresh white breadcrumbs
40 g/1$\frac{1}{2}$ oz butter
150 ml/$\frac{1}{4}$ pint single cream
salt and pepper
nutmeg to taste

Stick the cloves into the onion and put it in a saucepan with the bay leaf, parsley and milk. Cover and bring slowly to the boil. Remove from the heat and infuse for 30 minutes. Strain, discarding the onion and herbs.

Stir the breadcrumbs and butter into the milk, then cook very gently (use a double saucepan if possible) for 15 minutes. Stir in the cream and add salt, pepper and grated nutmeg to taste. It is important that the sauce is neither too thick nor too bland. Serve with roast turkey, chicken or pheasant. **Serves 8**

Cranberry Sauce

225 g/8 oz fresh cranberries
75 g/3 oz caster sugar
150 ml/$\frac{1}{4}$ pint fresh orange juice
large pinch of mixed spice
a little grated orange rind (optional)
1 tablespoon Cointreau or orange liqueur

Put all the ingredients except the orange rind and Cointreau or liqueur into a saucepan and stir well. Cook gently until the cranberries are soft — about 5 minutes. Stir in the orange rind and cointreau just before serving with roast turkey or game.

The cranberry sauce can be made a couple of days in advance and, when cooled, kept in a covered jar in the refrigerator. **Serves 8**

Opposite page Three Fish Kedgeree (page 71) and
Turkey Lasagne (page 74)
Overleaf Glazed Ham with Orange Sauce (page 44), Special-occasion
Lobster (page 31) and Chicken and Peach Salad (page 35)

Breakfasts and Brunches

There are those who ignore breakfast, those who loathe it and those who cannot face the day without it.

If you are entertaining a lot over Christmas and don't want to be tied to the kitchen stove from the moment you wake up, then try having your special meal in the evening, let everyone sleep late (including yourself) and settle for brunch. By combining breakfast and lunch you can save yourself a great deal of work.

Here are my ideas for super brunches to satisfy the breakfast addicts.

Opposite page Nanette with a breakfast tray of Ham and Cheese on Toast (page 77) and Breakfast Muffins (page 84)

A Victorian Salmon Soufflé

(Illustrated on page 148)

1 kg/2 lb fresh salmon
300 ml/½ pint double cream
2 teaspoons horseradish sauce
6 egg whites
salt and pepper
2 tablespoons chopped chives or a little dill weed

Remove the skin and bones from the salmon. Cut the flesh into cubes and purée it in a liquidiser or food processor with the cream and horseradish sauce. Chill for 15 minutes. Lightly whisk two of the egg whites and beat them into the mixture. Season to taste, then chill until the soufflé is to be cooked (the mixture will keep for up to 6 hours).

Set the oven at moderately hot (200 C, 400 F, gas 6). Stiffly whisk the rest of the egg whites and fold them into the salmon mixture with the chives or dill weed. Grease a 1.15-litre/2-pint soufflé dish and spoon the mixture into it. Stand the soufflé dish in a roasting tin half filled with hot water and bake in the heated oven for 50 to 60 minutes. When cooked the soufflé should be slightly soft in the centre. Serve with a Hollandaise Sauce (see Vegetable Terrine, page 54) to which some peeled cooked shrimps have been added. **Serves 8**

Smoked Salmon with Scrambled Eggs

12 large eggs
150 ml/¼ pint single or double cream
salt
cayenne pepper
50 g/2 oz butter
175 g/6 oz smoked salmon pieces or trimmings, chopped

Beat the eggs with half the cream, a little salt and cayenne to taste. Melt the butter in a large, heavy-based saucepan. Add the egg mixture and cook very slowly, stirring constantly, until the mixture is just set. Stir in the smoked salmon and remaining cream and serve immediately with brown bread and butter. **Serves 6**

Three Fish Kedgeree

(Illustrated on page 65)

100 g/4 oz butter
450 g/1 lb white or brown rice, cooked
1 teaspoon curry powder (or to taste)
175 g/6 oz peeled cooked prawns
100 g/4 oz cooked smoked haddock, free from skin and bone,
and flaked
225 g/8 oz cooked monk fish, cod or trout, flaked (free from
skin and bone)
4 hard-boiled eggs, quartered
300 ml/½ pint single or double cream
2 tablespoons chopped chives
salt and pepper

Heat the butter in a large heavy-based saucepan. Stir in the rice and curry powder and cook over a low heat until heated through. Stir in the prawns, smoked haddock and white fish or trout. Cover and leave over a very low heat until the fish is hot.

Stir in the eggs, cream and chives, then taste the mixture and adjust the seasoning. Serve immediately. **Serves 6**

Superb Salmon Fish Cakes with Spicy Sauce

450 g/1 lb fresh salmon
½ onion, sliced
1 tablespoon vinegar
1 bay leaf
4 peppercorns
salt and pepper
225 g/8 oz potatoes
2 egg yolks
1 tablespoon tomato ketchup
1 teaspoon anchovy essence (optional)
3 tablespoons flour, seasoned
1 egg, beaten
175 g/6 oz fresh white breadcrumbs
oil for shallow frying
TO SERVE
Home-made Tomato Sauce (page 63)
Tabasco sauce to taste
1 bag salted crisps

Put the salmon in a saucepan. Add water to cover, the onion slices, vinegar, bay leaf, peppercorns and a generous pinch of salt. Cover and bring to the boil, then reduce the heat and simmer gently for 5 minutes. Turn off the heat and let the salmon cool in the liquid.

Meanwhile, boil the potatoes until tender. Drain thoroughly and sieve or mash until very smooth. Drain and flake the cooled fish, removing all the skin and bones, then beat the fish into the potatoes with the egg yolks, tomato ketchup, anchovy essence and seasoning to taste.

Divide the mixture into 8 portions and shape each into a round cake, 2.5 cm/1 in thick. Coat the fish cakes in seasoned flour, then dip them in the beaten egg and finally roll them in breadcrumbs. Chill or freeze until ready to cook.

Heat a little oil in a heavy-based frying pan and shallow fry the fish cakes until crisp and golden brown – about 4 minutes on each side. Drain on absorbent kitchen paper.

To serve, heat the tomato sauce and add Tabasco to taste. Crush the crisps slightly and tip them on to a heated serving plate. Arrange the fish cakes on top and serve the sauce separately. **Serves 4 to 6**

Turkey Hash

4 tablespoons oil
2 large onions, thinly sliced
675 g/1½ lb cooked turkey, cut into strips
1 clove garlic, crushed (optional)
4 stalks celery, cut into strips
1 green pepper, deseeded and cut into strips
1 red pepper, deseeded and cut into strips
1 yellow pepper, deseeded and cut into strips
300 ml/½ pint soured cream
salt and pepper
1 medium beetroot, cooked, peeled and cut into strips
lemon slices to garnish

Heat the oil in a large heavy-based frying pan, add the onions and fry until golden brown. Stir in the turkey and garlic (if used) with the celery and peppers, and stir-fry for several minutes to lightly cook the vegetables. Stir in the soured cream and seasoning to taste. Allow to heat through, then carefully stir in the beetroot. Serve immediately garnished, if you like, with slices of lemon. **Serves 4 to 6**

Turkey Lasagne

(Illustrated on page 65)

A different way to eat up leftover turkey.

1 kg/2 lb cooked, boneless turkey meat, minced or chopped
1 red pepper, cored and cut into fine strips
100 g/4 oz blanched almonds, toasted or fried
175 g/6 oz lasagne verdi sheets (those which do not require
pre-cooking)
100 g/4 oz mozzarella cheese, thinly sliced
SAUCE
75 g/3 oz butter
40 g/1½ oz flour
600 ml/1 pint milk
150 ml/¼ pint single cream
½ teaspoon mustard powder, or to taste
juice from crushing 1 clove garlic
100 g/4 oz Gruyère or Cheddar cheese, grated
salt and pepper

Grease a large oblong shallow ovenproof baking dish. Mix the turkey
with the red pepper and the almonds.

Make the sauce: melt the butter in a large saucepan, stir in the flour,
then gradually mix in the milk. Bring to the boil, stirring constantly,
until smooth and quite thick. Simmer for a minute.

Remove the saucepan from the heat, and stir in the cream, mustard,
garlic juice, cheese and seasoning to taste. Stir the turkey mixture into
the sauce and spoon a layer of it into the prepared dish, then cover with a
layer of lasagne. Continue layering up the lasagne and sauce in this way
until all the ingredients have been used, finishing with a layer of the
sauce mixture. Top with the mozzarella cheese, then bake in a moderate
oven (180 C, 350 F, gas 4) for 40 to 45 minutes, or until golden brown.
Serves 8

Beef and Rice 'Lasagne'

2 tablespoons oil
2 medium onions, finely chopped
2 cloves garlic, crushed (or to taste)
1 kg/2 lb chuck steak, minced
1 kg/2 lb tomatoes, peeled, quartered and deseeded
2 tablespoons Worcestershire sauce
(or to taste)
3 tablespoons tomato purée (or to taste)
1 beef stock cube
salt and pepper
50 g/2 oz butter
50 g/2 oz flour
600 ml/1 pint milk
225 g/8 oz cheese (Cheddar, Gruyère or similar), grated
450 g/1 lb cooked long-grain rice (brown or white)

Grease a large oblong shallow ovenproof baking dish. Heat the oil in a large heavy-based saucepan; cook the onions and garlic slowly until soft. Add the beef and stir-fry over high heat until browned. Reduce the heat and stir in the tomatoes, Worcestershire sauce, purée, stock cube and seasoning. Simmer gently, stirring frequently, for 15 minutes.

Make a cheese sauce by melting the butter in a saucepan, stir in the flour, then gradually add the milk, stirring continuously, until smooth. Bring to the boil, stirring continuously, and cook until thick and smooth. Season to taste and stir in 175 g/6 oz of the grated cheese.

Spread half of the meat mixture in the baking dish. Cover with the cooked rice, then the remaining meat mixture. Spoon the cheese sauce on top and sprinkle with the remaining cheese. Bake in a moderate oven (180 c, 350 f, gas 4) for 30 to 40 minutes, until golden and bubbling.
Serves 6

Breakfast Kebabs

For a brunch party allow 2 kebabs per person.

Bacon Specials

12 rindless rashers streaky bacon
100 g/4 oz button mushrooms
8 prunes (those which do not require pre-soaking)
100 g/4 oz Gruyère or Edam cheese
a little oil

Roll up the bacon rashers; wipe and trim the mushrooms, then remove the stones from the prunes. Cut the cheese into eight cubes and press a cube of cheese in the centre of each prune.

Thread the bacon, mushrooms and prunes on to four skewers. Brush the kebabs with a little oil and cook under a hot grill, turning frequently, until the bacon is crisp and golden brown – about 5 minutes. **Serves 4**

Note: These kebabs can be prepared in advance and chilled ready for cooking next day.

Skewered Avocado with Sausage and Bacon

2 firm (but ripe) avocado pears
1 tablespoon oil
1 tablespoon lemon juice
cayenne pepper *or* Tabasco sauce
14 rindless rashers streaky bacon
12 cocktail sausages

Peel and stone the avocados, then cut each one into eight chunks. Mix the oil, lemon juice and cayenne or Tabasco and brush this mixture over the avocado chunks. Stretch the bacon with the back of a knife. Cut each rasher in half and wrap all the avocado chunks and cocktail sausages individually in a piece of bacon. Thread the prepared rolls alternately on to four skewers, beginning and ending each skewer with avocado rolls. Cook the kebabs under a hot grill, turning frequently, until golden brown and thoroughly cooked – about 5 minutes. **Makes 4 kebabs**

Ham and Cheese on Toast

(Illustrated on page 68)

allow 1 slice each of bread and lean cooked ham per person
CHEESE SAUCE
4 tablespoons butter
4 tablespoons flour
250 ml/8 fl oz milk
salt and pepper
1 egg yolk
225 g/8 oz Gruyère or Cheddar cheese, grated
GARNISH
tomato slices
sprigs of parsley

Toast the slices of bread and place a slice of ham on each. To make the sauce, melt the butter in a pan and stir in the flour. Add the milk and whisk over a medium heat until smooth and boiling. Add salt, pepper and the egg yolk. Stir until thoroughly mixed, then remove from the heat. Add the grated cheese and stir until it has melted.

Pour the cheese mixture over the slices of toast and ham and place them under a hot grill until golden brown. Garnish each portion with a slice of tomato and parsley. **Serves 4 to 6**

Egg in a Bun

6 granary buns or crisp breakfast rolls
50 g/2 oz butter, softened
75 g/3 oz rindless rashers bacon, cooked and crumbled
3 eggs · 225 g/8 oz Gruyère cheese, grated

Scoop out the middle of each bun, then butter the inside of each one and stand them on a baking tray. Bake in a moderate oven (180 c, 350 F, gas 4) for 5 minutes, then remove from the oven and place a little of the bacon inside each bun.

Crack an egg into each bun and sprinkle the grated cheeese on top, then return to the oven for 15 to 20 minutes, or until the egg is cooked to taste. Serve immediately. **Serves 6**

Variation

Egg in Tomato: Allow 1 large beef steak tomato and 1 egg per person. Cut the top off the tomato and scoop out the middle, then leave the shell to drain for a few minutes (upside-down on absorbent kitchen paper). Break an egg into the tomato shell, add seasoning and 1 tablespoon single cream, then top with grated cheese. Bake as above and serve immediately, with triangles of fried bread if you like.

Sensational Brunch

(Illustrated on page 85)

For three or four people use six to eight eggs. Peel and thinly slice one large tomato, slice two or three mushrooms and chop a couple of spring onions. Put the vegetables in a pot, season and cook lightly. Grate some Cheddar cheese into a non-stick saucepan and melt it slowly, then break the eggs into it. When the whites start to set, stir and dump in the warm vegetables. Stir continuously until the whole slop sets, then serve it on toast.

This is Roger Moore's invention – he often makes it for lunch in his caravan when he's on location filming. His method of cooking is unorthodox (so is the way he writes the recipe) but all his friends agree it tastes delicious.

Spinach Soufflé

100 ml/4 fl oz mayonnaise
50 g/2 oz plain flour
300 ml/½ pint milk
100 g/4 oz Cheddar cheese, grated
salt and pepper
275 g/10 oz thoroughly drained, cooked spinach
4 egg yolks, lightly beaten
5 egg whites

Try using cooked broccoli instead of spinach, chopping it in the food processor first.

Set the oven at moderate (160 c, 325 f, gas 3). Butter a 1.75-litre/3-pint soufflé dish and make a collar of double thickness greaseproof paper to fit around it. Secure the paper in place with string. The collar should rise at least 7.5 cm/3 in above the rim of the dish.

Combine the mayonnaise with the flour in a saucepan, then gradually add the milk and stir over a low heat until the mixture thickens. Off the heat, stir in the grated cheese, seasoning and cooked spinach. Mix in the egg yolks. Whisk the egg whites until they stand in stiff peaks, then fold them into the soufflé.

Turn into the prepared dish and bake in the heated oven for about 40 to 60 minutes, or until the soufflé is well risen. Serve immediately.
Serves 4 to 6

Bread and Cheese Brunch

15 g/½ oz butter
8 slices bread, crusts removed
450 g/1 lb Cheddar cheese, grated
600 ml/1 pint milk
3 eggs
1 teaspoon rubbed sage
salt and pepper

Line the base of a buttered ovenproof dish with half the bread, then sprinkle half the cheese on top in a thick layer. Top with the remaining bread and sprinkle the rest of the cheese on top.

Beat the milk, eggs, sage and seasoning together, then pour this mixture over the bread and cheese and leave in the refrigerator for a few hours (or overnight) so that the liquid really soaks into the bread.

Bake in a moderate oven (180 c, 350 f, gas 4) for 1 hour, until crisp and golden. Serve immediately. **Serves 6**

Alsace Onion Tart

8 individual pastry shells (see Small Quiches, page 24)
4 tablespoons oil
450 g/1 lb strong onions, chopped
1 bay leaf
sprig of fresh thyme
salt and pepper
150 ml/$\frac{1}{4}$ pint dry Alsatian wine
2 eggs
200 ml/7 fl oz single cream

Prepare and cook the pastry shells according to the recipe instructions. Heat a baking tray in the oven.

Heat the oil in a non-stick frying pan. Add the onions, bay leaf, thyme and seasoning, then cover and cook gently until the onions are soft and transparent. Add the wine and simmer, uncovered, until all the liquid has evaporated. Remove the bay leaf and thyme and taste for seasoning. Whisk the eggs and cream together.

Divide the onions between the quiche shells and pour in the egg mixture. Place on the hot baking sheet and bake in a moderately hot oven (190 c, 375 f, gas 5) for 15 minutes. Serve hot or cold. **Serves 8**

The Alternative Sandwich

1 large unsliced loaf

TURKEY FILLING

225 g/8 oz cooked turkey, finely chopped
2 sticks celery
75 g/3 oz cream cheese
3 tablespoons mayonnaise
1 teaspoon Dijon mustard
salt and pepper

CHEESE AND WATERCRESS FILLING

1 bunch watercress, trimmed and very finely chopped
75 g/3 oz cream cheese
75 g/3 oz Cheddar cheese, grated
2 tablespoons mayonnaise
1 tablespoon finely chopped walnuts

HAM FILLING

75 g/3 oz cream cheese
3 tablespoons mayonnaise
75 g/3 oz lean cooked ham, finely chopped
1 tablespoon finely chopped parsley

Mix the ingredients for the different fillings in separate bowls, cover and set aside. Remove all the crusts from the loaf and cut the bread horizontally into four thick slices.

Spread each of three slices thickly with one of the filling mixtures, then sandwich the slices back together again and top with the fourth slice of bread. Sprinkle with chopped herbs and wrap the loaf tightly in cling film. Chill in the refrigerator for a few hours, then serve cut into slices, with your favourite chutney as an accompaniment. **Serves 6**

Home-made Cereal

4 handfuls oatmeal
1 large handful desiccated coconut
1 small handful mixed nuts
1 tablespoon sunflower seeds
1 tablespoon bran
50 g/2 oz demerara sugar
2 teaspoons clear honey

Mix all the ingredients and spread the cereal evenly in a lightly oiled baking tin. Bake in a moderate oven (180 C, 350 F, gas 4) until brown and crunchy, stirring it up every few minutes. Cool and store in an airtight jar.

Eat with yogurt or milk, for a healthy breakfast, or on its own as a snack while waiting for the turkey to cook. You could also give it to a health-conscious friend in a pretty jar as a gift. **Serves 2**

Banana Bread

100 g/4 oz butter
225 g/8 oz soft brown sugar
1 egg
2 ripe bananas, mashed
225 g/8 oz plain flour
1 teaspoon salt
1½ teaspoons baking powder
4 tablespoons yogurt

Beat the butter and sugar together until creamy, then beat in the egg. Mix in the mashed bananas. Sift together the flour, salt and baking powder. Mix half the yogurt into the creamed butter and sugar, then add half the flour mixture. Next mix in the rest of the yogurt and finally the rest of the flour.

Grease a 450-g/1-lb loaf tin, turn the bread mixture into it and bake in a moderate oven (180 C, 350 F, gas 4) for 1 hour, or until the loaf sounds hollow when tapped on the underside. Leave to cool on a wire rack. **Makes one 450-g/1-lb loaf**

Quick Walnut Bread

(Illustrated on page 85)

1.4 kg/3 lb wholemeal flour
$\frac{1}{2}$ teaspoon salt
25 g/1 oz fresh yeast *or* 15 g/$\frac{1}{2}$ oz dried yeast
1 litre/1$\frac{3}{4}$ pints lukewarm water
1$\frac{1}{2}$ teaspoons honey
175 g/6 oz walnuts, chopped

Mix the flour with the salt in a large, warmed mixing bowl. Mix the yeast with a third of the water and the honey. Leave in a warm place for about 10 minutes, or until frothy. Gradually work the yeast liquid into the flour with the remaining water, adding a little more water if necessary, to make a soft but not sticky dough. Knead thoroughly for 5 minutes or until the dough is smooth and elastic. Knead in the walnuts.

Divide the dough in half and shape each piece into a loaf. Place in greased 1-kg/2-lb loaf tins, cover and leave in a warm place until the dough has risen to the top of each tin. Bake in a hot oven (230 c, 450 f, gas 8) for 5 minutes, then reduce the temperature to (200 c, 400 f, gas 6) and bake for a further 30 minutes.

To test whether the bread is cooked, turn it out of the tin and tap the loaf on the bottom: when the bread is cooked it should sound hollow. Cool on a wire tack. **Makes two 1-kg/2-lb loaves**

Note: This bread can be frozen.

Breakfast Muffins

(Illustrated on page 68)

150 g/5 oz self-raising flour
100 g/4 oz wholemeal flour
100 g/4 oz muesli
100 g/4 oz soft brown sugar
3 teaspoons baking powder
$\frac{1}{4}$ teaspoon salt
1 egg, beaten
300 ml/$\frac{1}{2}$ pint milk
50 ml/2 fl oz sunflower oil
75 g/3 oz raisins

Stir the flours, muesli, sugar, baking powder and salt together in a large mixing bowl and make a well in the middle. In another bowl beat all the liquid ingredients together, then pour them into the flour mixture. Gradually mix the dry and liquid ingredients together and fold in the raisins. Mix thoroughly.

Spoon the mixture into 12 or 15 greased muffin tins, leaving a small space at the top of each tin. Bake in a moderately hot oven (200 c, 400 f, gas 6) for 20 to 25 minutes.

Allow the muffins to cool slightly in their tins before turning them out on to a wire rack. Serve while still warm with butter and honey.
Makes 12 to 15

Try a handful of walnuts or any crunchy health food cereal instead of muesli, or use chopped prunes, apples, bananas or apricots instead of raisins. Let the children make these because whatever they do this recipe never fails.

Opposite page Sensational Brunch (page 78), Quick Walnut Bread
(page 83) and Special Whisky Preserve (page 143)
Overleaf Nanette in the kitchen with daughters Sarah (left)
and Emma

Just Desserts

While on the subject of these utterly delicious, calorie-ridden temptations, why not try inviting friends over for coffee and dessert instead of the usual pre-dinner cocktails? Then you needn't worry about what is burning in the kitchen when a friend lingers for yet another drink — you can relax and indulge yourself for a change in the happy knowledge that the fire brigade is not going to be called out!

Opposite page Maraschino Cherry Ice Cream (page 103) and Brown Bread Ice Cream (page 102) in Flower Ice Bowls (page 104)

Christmas Pudding

This delicious, fruity yet light pudding, made without flour, is more digestible than traditional rich and heavy puddings.

225 g/8 oz wholemeal breadcrumbs
50 g/2 oz ground almonds
pinch of salt
1 heaped teaspoon ground mixed spice
100 g/4 oz dark soft brown sugar
100 g/4 oz figs, chopped
225 g/8 oz blanched almonds, cut into slivers
100 g/4 oz pine kernels
100 g/4 oz stoned dates, chopped
100 g/4 oz currants
100 g/4 oz sultanas
225 g/8 oz seedless raisins
100 g/4 oz candied peel, chopped
1 large cooking apple,
peeled, cored and finely chopped
100 g/4 oz butter, softened
grated rind and juice of 1 lemon
100 g/4 oz set honey
3 eggs, beaten
4 tablespoons brandy

In a large bowl, mix the breadcrumbs, ground almonds, salt, spice, sugar, figs, slivered almonds, pine kernels, dates, the currants, sultanas, raisins, candied peel and the chopped apple.

Cream the butter with the lemon rind and juice and the honey. Gradually beat in the eggs and the brandy. Stir this mixture into the dry ingredients. When thoroughly mixed, spoon into two 1-kg/2-lb greased pudding basins. Cover with greased greaseproof paper, then cover closely with cooking foil and tie with string. Steam the puddings for 3 hours. Make sure that the water does not evaporate completely during cooking and top up with extra water as necessary.

Allow to cool, then replace the greaseproof paper and foil with fresh covering. Store in a cool dry place. On Christmas day, steam the pudding for a further 3 hours. Turn out the pudding on to a heated serving dish and pour some warmed brandy over it. Immediately set alight and serve while flaming. Serve with Brandy Butter (page 117) or cream. **Each pudding serves 8**

Incredible Rice Pudding

100 g/4 oz sultanas · 2 tablespoons rum
50 g/2 oz round-grain rice
450 ml/¾ pint milk · 25 g/1 oz butter
1 tablespoon double cream
2 eggs, separated · 50 g/2 oz sugar
pinch each of salt and nutmeg
150 ml/1¼ pint double cream, whipped (optional)

Leave the sultanas to soak in the rum for as long as you wish.

Cook the rice in the milk until just tender (7 minutes), then stir in the butter and cream. Lightly beat the egg yolks and slowly stir in the rice, followed by the sugar, sultanas and rum, salt and nutmeg. Cool.

Whisk the egg whites until stiff, fold into the rice mixture and pour into an ovenproof dish. Stand this in a roasting tin half filled with hot water and bake in a moderate oven (160c, 325 f, gas 3) for 30 minutes, or until firm to the touch. This rice pudding is great whether served hot or cold. For those who don't count calories, allow the pudding to cool, then fold in the whipped cream and serve in wine glasses – is worth starving next day for this! **Serves 6**

A Different
Bread and Butter Pudding

50 g/2 oz butter
10 slices from a large loaf of white bread
275 g/10 oz sultanas · 2 bananas, sliced
6 eggs · 175 g/6 oz sugar
6 tablespoons rum · 1.15 litres/2 pints milk

Grease a large, not too deep, ovenproof dish. Butter the slices of bread and layer them with the sultanas and bananas. Beat the eggs, sugar, rum and milk together and pour over the bread, then chill for 1 hour so that the mixture becomes really moist.

Bake in a moderate oven (180c, 350f, gas 4) for 45 to 60 minutes. Serve hot for a really sustaining pudding. **Serves 10 to 12**

Eating at Shakira and Mike Caine's house is always great, particularly the Sunday lunches. One Sunday they cooked bread and butter pudding with a difference — even bread and butter pudding haters were converted.

Cloutie Dumpling

(Illustrated on pages 46/47)

*This is a traditional Scottish celebration pudding, although it is
frequently served cold, sliced like a cake. The name is derived from
the fact that the pudding is cooked in a cloth or 'cloutie'. Serve as a
Christmas pudding with cream, custard or brandy butter.*

350 g/12 oz plain flour
100 g/4 oz fresh white breadcrumbs
225 g/8 oz shredded suet
225 g/8 oz dark soft brown sugar
1 teaspooon baking powder
1 teaspoon mixed spice
1 teaspoon ground ginger
$\frac{1}{2}$ teaspoon cinnamon
1 tablespoon golden syrup
1 tablespoon marmalade
3 tablespoons black treacle
1 tablespoon milk
2 large carrots, grated
575 g/1$\frac{1}{4}$ lbs dried mixed fruit
2 large eggs, beaten

Mix all the ingredients together to make a fairly firm mixture. Put a
clean pudding cloth, or large clean tea-towel, into a pan of boiling water
and boil for 1 minute. Drain and when cool enough to handle, squeeze
dry. Spread on a work surface and liberally sprinkle with flour: this
forms the important seal or crust around the pudding during boiling.
Spoon the mixture into the middle of the cloth and shape it into a neat
round. Gather up the cloth and tie securely leaving room for the
pudding to swell slightly. Bring a large saucepan of water to the boil.
Put the dumpling into the pan, standing it on a trivet or an upturned
saucer, cover and boil for 3 hours, topping up the water when necessary.

Remove from the pan, and leave the dumpling to stand for 5 minutes
before removing the cloth. Serve hot, cut into slices. **Serves 8**

Tarte Tatin

(Illustrated on pages 106/107)

225 g/8 oz plain flour
100 g/4 oz butter, chilled and diced
50 g/2 oz walnuts, ground
100 g/4 oz sugar
2 egg yolks
FILLING
75 g/3 oz butter
175 g/6 oz sugar
1–1.5 kg/2–3 lb Golden Delicious apples, peeled, cored and
halved

Sift the flour into a bowl, then rub in the butter until the mixture resembles fine breadcrumbs. Stir in the walnuts and sugar and work in the egg yolks to make a pastry dough. Wrap and chill the pastry while you prepare the filling.

For the tarte tatin you will need a shallow flameproof dish or pan. Ideally a cast iron frying pan, with a handle short enough for the pan to fit in the oven; alternatively a flameproof gratin dish will do. Melt the butter and sugar together in the pan, then arrange the apple halves, packed closely together, standing upright on top of the sugar. The apples should fill the pan. Cook gently for about 20 minutes, or until the sugar forms a golden caramel. Remove from the heat and cool.

Roll out the pastry into a sheet large enough to cover the apples, with a little extra to tuck in round the sides. Lift the pastry over the apples and tuck the edges in neatly. Prick the dough all over with a fork, then bake in a moderately hot oven (190 c, 375 F, gas 5) for about 30 to 35 minutes or until the pastry is cooked. Cool until just warm in the pan, then place a serving plate over the top of the pan and invert the tarte tatin on to it. Serve warm. **Serves 6**

Boxing Day Alternative Pudding

6 oranges · 4 pink grapefruit
2 white grapefruit · 4 tangerines
chopped mint

Slice all the skin and pith from the citrus fruits. Slice the flesh as thinly as possible. Arrange the prepared fruit in a large dish, overlapping the slices: start with the tangerines in the middle, then the white and pink grapefruit and the oranges. Pour over any orange juice that may have escaped in the slicing and sprinkle with chopped mint. Cover with cling film until needed.

This salad is ideal for Christmas dieters or for those who would like a change from rich food. Serve any leftover fruit for breakfast next day. **Serves 8**

Rich Carrot Dessert

6 eggs, separated
175 g/6 oz soft brown sugar
325 g/12 oz puréed cooked carrots
1 tablespoon grated orange rind
1 tablespoon grated lemon rind
1 tablespoon brandy
350 g/12 oz ground almonds
50 g/2 oz self-raising flour · 1 carrot, grated
1 teaspoon fresh or frozen orange juice

This is meant to be a bit soggy, so don't panic – it tastes wonderful.

Line and grease a deep 22-cm/8½-in cake tin. Beat the egg yolks with the brown sugar until pale and thick. Add the puréed carrots, grated rinds, brandy, almonds, flour, grated carrot and fruit juice and gently fold the ingredients together until thoroughly mixed.

Beat the egg whites until stiff and fold them into the rest of the ingredients. Pour into the prepared cake tin and bake in a moderate oven (160 C, 325 F, gas 3) for 50 minutes or until a skewer comes out clean from the centre of the cake. Cool slightly in the tin, before turning out on to a wire rack. **Serves 8**

Note: This can also be served as an unusual cake to have at teatime.

Eli's Cheesecake

75 g/3 oz butter
275 g/10 oz sugar
250 g/8½ oz chocolate digestive biscuits, crushed
¼ teaspoon nutmeg
175 g/6 oz walnuts, ground
4 eggs
675 g/1½ lb cream cheese
100 ml/4 fl oz soured cream
1 teaspoon vanilla essence
pinch of salt
350 g/12 oz chocolate chips
DECORATION
curls of chocolate
icing sugar

Melt the butter and 50 g/2 oz of the sugar together, mix in the crushed biscuits, nutmeg and ground walnuts, then press this mixture into the base of a 30-cm/12-in loose-bottomed cake tin and leave to set.

Whisk the eggs with the remaining sugar until pale and thick. Beat in the cream cheese until smooth, fold in the soured cream, vanilla essence, pinch of salt and chocolate chips and mix thoroughly. Pour the mixture over the biscuit base and bake in a moderate oven (180 C, 350 F, gas 4) for 1 hour, or until firm to touch.

Leave the cheesecake to cool before removing it from the tin, then refrigerate until required. Decorate with curls of chocolate and dust with icing sugar. **Serves 12**

When Bryan was making a film in Chicago, we often ate at a famous restaurant called 'Eli's Steak House'. To round off every meal, Eli offers a selection of devastating cheesecakes. I persuaded him to part with the secret of this chocolate chip cheesecake - a dessert so calorie-laden that it doesn't bear thinking about. So don't think about it, just enjoy it.

My Cheesecake

100 g/4 oz digestive biscuits, crushed
75 g/3 oz, plus 1 tablespoon, caster sugar
50 g/2 oz butter, melted
1 teaspoon ground cinnamon
450 g/1 lb Philadelphia cream cheese
2 large eggs, beaten
few drops of vanilla essence
TOPPING
300 ml/½ pint soured cream
1 tablespoon caster sugar
few drops of vanilla essence

If you want an extra creamy cheesecake, add a small carton of double cream to the Philadelphia cheese.

Grease a 20-cm/8-in springform tin. Mix the biscuits, 1 tablespoon caster sugar, melted butter and cinnamon. Press into the base of the tin and chill while preparing the filling. Beat the cheese until smooth, then beat in the remaining ingredients. Pour over the base and place in a moderately hot oven (190 c, 375 f, gas 5). Bake for 25 minutes. Remove the cheesecake from the oven and increase the heat to very hot (240 c, 475 f, gas 9). Mix all the topping ingredients together and carefully spread the mixture over the top of the cheesecake. Replace in the oven for exactly 5 minutes. Remove, allow to cool, then chill overnight.
Serves 6 to 8

Chocolate Roulade

(Illustrated on pages 106/107)

175 g/6 oz plain chocolate
5 eggs, separated
150 g/5 oz caster sugar
75 g/3 oz plain flour
600 ml/1 pint double cream, whipped
2 tablespoons rum
1 tablespoon icing sugar

Melt the cholate in a bowl over hot water. In a mixing bowl, beat the egg yolks with the sugar until thick, light and creamy.

In another bowl, whisk the egg whites until stiff. Fold the flour, melted chocolate and egg whites into the sugar and yolk mixture. Pour the mixture into a lined and greased Swiss roll tin measuring 23 cm × 33 cm/9 × 13 in. Bake for 10 to 12 minutes in a moderately hot oven (190 c, 375 f, gas 5).

Remove the roulade from the oven, cover with a damp cloth and leave until cooled. Turn the cake out on to greaseproof paper which has been liberally sprinkled with icing sugar.

Whip 300 ml/½ pint of the cream with the rum and icing sugar and spread this evenly over the cake. Roll up the cake, then cover with the remainder of the cream, whipped until thick. Decorate by marking the cream along the length of the roulade with a fork.

Chill the cake until ready for serving, decorated with holly and sprinkled with icing sugar. **Serves 6**

Prune and Apricot Pie

BASE
75 g/3 oz butter
50 g/2 oz sugar
225 g/8 oz digestive biscuits, crushed
FILLING
2 (225-g/8-oz) packets Philadelphia cream cheese
about 3 tablespoons icing sugar, sifted (or to taste)
2 tablespoons frozen concentrated orange juice
225 g/8 oz prunes, cooked and stoned
250 ml/8 oz double cream
225 g/8 oz dried apricots, cooked
flaked almonds, toasted, to decorate

To make the base, melt the butter over low heat then mix in the sugar and crushed biscuits. Press into the base and sides of a 20-cm/8-in loose-bottomed flan tin or pie plate and chill until firm.

For the filling, beat the cream cheese until smooth and soft, fold in the icing sugar, adding more to your taste if you like, and orange juice. Spread the mixture in the pie crust and refrigerate until set. Meanwhile, purée the prunes. Whip 150 ml/¼ pint of the cream until thick and fold in the prune purée. Purée the apricots too, whip the rest of the cream until thick and fold in the apricot purée.

Remove the crust from the tin or leave it in the pie plate and swirl the prune mixture around the outer edge of the pie, leaving a hole in the centre. Swirl the apricot mixture in the centre and decorate with toasted flaked almonds. **Serves 6 to 8**

Pecan Pie

This is an authentic southern-style nut pie from the States.

PASTRY
225 g/8 oz plain flour
pinch each of salt and baking powder
1 teaspoon caster sugar
150 g/5 oz butter or block margarine, chilled
1 egg yolk · 3–4 tablespoons milk
FILLING
3 large eggs
175 g/6 oz golden syrup, warmed
100 g/4 oz black treacle, warmed *or* soft brown sugar
65 g/2½ oz butter, melted and cooled
grated rind and juice of 1 lemon
225 g/8 oz pecan halves

Set the oven at moderate (180 c, 350 f, gas 4) and place a baking tray in the oven to heat.

To make the pastry, sift the flour, salt and baking powder into a bowl and add the sugar. Dice the butter or margarine, add to the flour mixture and rub in using your fingertips until the mixture resembles fine breadcrumbs. Mix the egg yolk with the milk and mix into the dry ingredients to make a soft, but not sticky, dough. Add a little extra milk if the mixture is too dry. Turn out on to a floured surface and knead lightly. Roll out and use to line a 25-cm/10-in flan tin. Chill.

For the filling, lightly beat the eggs until they are frothy, then stir in the golden syrup, black treacle or sugar, butter and lemon rind and juice. Mix well. Arrange the pecans in the base of the flan and pour over the egg mixture. Place the flan on the hot baking sheet and bake in the heated oven for 1 hour or until set. Cool and serve with ice-cream.
Serves 8

Melon and Lychees

Using a melon scoop, remove all the flesh from a ripe Israeli melon. Mix the melon with a (227-g/8-oz) can of lychees (drained) adding a dash of the juice from the can and chill for 30 minutes before serving. Arrange in individual glass dishes, or in the melon halves, and decorate with mint sprigs. If you like you can sprinkle the fruit with a little gin. **Serves 4**

Gratin of Pancakes

The pancakes can be made ahead and frozen.
You can replace the fruit with Luxurious Mincemeat (page 144).
Serve with ice cream.

PANCAKES
100 g/4 oz plain flour
1 egg
450 ml/¾ pint milk
1 teaspoon sugar
1 tablespoon melted butter
FILLING
225 g/8 oz Philadelphia cheese
75 g/3 oz caster sugar
grated rind and juice of 1 lemon
1 banana, thinly sliced
2 kiwis, thinly sliced
3 slices fresh or canned pineapple, chopped
2 oranges, peeled and cut into segments
3 tablespoons chopped almonds or hazelnuts, lightly toasted
TOPPING
4 egg yolks
100 g/4 oz caster sugar
3 tablespoons brandy, sherry or rum

To make the pancakes, sift the flour into a bowl. Gradually beat in the egg and milk until a smooth batter is formed. Stir in the sugar and butter and, if possible, leave the batter to stand for a couple of hours. Cook the pancakes in a heavy-based or non-stick frying pan, using a little melted butter or oil to prevent them from sticking to the pan. Stack the cooked pancakes on a plate with sheets of greaseproof paper between them to prevent them from sticking together. You will need ten pancakes for the gratin.

To make the filling, cream the cheese with the sugar, lemon rind and juice. Gently warm the pancakes in a frying pan with a little butter. Stack the pancakes, layering them alternately with the cream cheese mixture and the fruit. Top with the nuts.

To make the topping whisk the egg yolks with the sugar and brandy until thick and frothy (this may be easier in a bowl over hot water, or in the top of a double boiler). Spoon this over the pancakes and place under a hot grill until golden brown and bubbling. Cut into wedges (like a cake) and serve. **Serves 4 to 6**

Snowballs

This is a recipe for baked apples.
If you use bought mincemeat instead of the home-made version on
page 144, add some brandy, slivered almonds, chopped walnuts or
crystallised fruits to the mixture with a little mixed spice.

6 large cooking apples · 6 tablespoons mincemeat
1 tablespoon pine kernels
100–175 g/4–6 oz Philadelphia cheese
265 g/9½ oz caster sugar
1 tablespoon brandy
4 egg whites
DECORATION
glacé cherries · angelica leaves

Peel and core the apples. Mix the mincemeat with the pine kernels; cream the cheese, 40 g/1½ oz of the sugar and brandy. Stand the apples in a shallow baking dish, placing them well apart, and spoon the mincemeat mixture into the central holes left by the cores. Top with the cheese mixture, smoothing it over the top of the apples.

Whisk the egg whites until they are stiff, then gradually whisk in half the remaining sugar, then fold in the remainder. Pipe or spoon the meringue over the apples to completely cover them. Bake in a moderate oven (180 c, 350 f, gas 4) for 1 hour, or until the apples are just tender and the topping golden brown.

Serve, decorated with glacé cherries and angelica leaves, with cream or ice cream. **Serves 6**

Chilled Orange Soufflé

2 tablespoons gelatine
300 ml/½ pint water · 8 eggs, separated
2 (175-ml/6-fl oz) cans frozen concentrated orange juice
200 g/7 oz caster sugar
450 ml/¾ pint double cream
2 tablespoons orange liqueur
2 tablespoons chopped blanched almonds, lightly toasted

First prepare a 1.15-litre/2-pint soufflé dish (see below). Sprinkle the gelatine over the water in a small bowl, set it aside for 5 minutes to soften, then dissolve it completely by stirring it over a saucepan of hot water. Set aside to cool. Beat the egg yolks until they are thick and pale, then whisk in the gelatine. Cook this mixture in its bowl over a saucepan of hot water, stirring continuously, until it has thickened enough to coat the back of a spoon. Take care not to boil the mixture, or to overcook it, or it will curdle. Remove from the heat and immediately stir in the orange juice. Chill for about 30 minutes, or until the mixture becomes syrupy in consistency.

Whisk the egg whites until they are foamy, then gradually pour in the sugar, whisking all the time, and continue to whisk until the mixture stands in stiff, glossy peaks. In a separate bowl, lightly whip 300 ml/ $\frac{1}{2}$ pint of the cream with the orange liqueur. Fold the egg whites into the cream.

Carefully fold the cream mixture into the chilled orange custard, then pour the soufflé mixture into the prepared dish and chill thoroughly until set. To serve, carefully remove the paper collar: do this by easing it away from the mixture with the blade of a long knife. Whip the remaining cream until it stands in peaks. Press the nuts around the sides of the soufflé if you like, then pipe the cream around the top. **Serves 6**

To prepare a soufflé dish: tie a wide band of double thickness greaseproof paper around the outside of the dish. It should be high enough to stand at least 7.5 cm/3 in above the rim of the dish. Secure the band of paper with a piece of sticky tape and string.

Chocolate Mousse

350 g/12 oz plain chocolate
150 g/5 oz butter · 7 egg yolks
4 tablespoons brandy, rum or Grand Marnier
CHOCOLATE LEAVES
100 g/4 oz plain chocolate
a few firm rose leaves

Melt the chocolate with the butter in the top of a double boiler or in a bowl over a saucepan of hot water. Beat in the egg yolks one at a time, then stir in the brandy, rum or Grand Marnier.

In a separate bowl, whisk the egg whites until they stand in stiff peaks, then fold them into the chocolate mixture. Pour or spoon the mousse into a glass serving dish or individual glass dishes and chill thoroughly; this mousse is best made the day before it is to be eaten, in which case the dishes should be covered with cling film when they are chilled.

To make the chocolate leaves for decoration, melt the chocolate in a double boiler or bowl over a saucepan of hot water. Spread or brush the chocolate over the leaves, on the side with the raised veins. Leave in a cool place until the chocolate has set, then carefully peel the leaves off and use the chocolate shapes to decorate the mousse. **Serves 6**

Brown Bread Ice Cream

(Illustrated on page 88)

Wendy, a friend I went to RADA with, gave me this recipe and it's always a success.

75 g/3 oz brown breadcrumbs
50 g/2 oz demerara sugar · 4 eggs, separated
300 ml/½ pint double cream
50 g/2 oz caster sugar

Mix the breadcrumbs and demerara sugar together, then grill them on the lowest setting until brown and crunchy (make sure they don't burn). Leave to cool.

Lightly beat the egg yolks. Whisk the double cream until thick. Finally whisk the egg whites to soft peaks and gradually whisk in the caster sugar until glossy. Fold all the ingredients together and freeze in a suitable container or an ice cream mould. **Serves 6**

Frozen Chestnut Pudding

(Illustrated on pages 106/107)

600 ml/1 pint double cream
175 g/6 oz caster sugar · 6 eggs, separated
100 g/4 oz canned chestnuts, drained and chopped
1 tablespoon rum
DECORATION
300 ml/½ pint whipping cream, whipped
4 canned chestnuts, drained and sliced

Whip the cream with a tablespoon of the sugar until thick; beat the egg yolks with 50 g/2 oz of the sugar until thick and light, then whisk the egg whites until stiff and gradually whisk in the remaining sugar. Gently mix the cream with the yolks and meringue mixture. Fold in the chestnuts and rum. Pack into a bombe mould or freezer-proof bowl and freeze until firm.

Dip the mould in hot water and turn out on to a plate. Decorate with cream and chestnut slices. Serve immediately. **Serves 8**

Maraschino Cherry Ice Cream

(Illustrated on page 88)

900 ml/1½ pints double cream
225 g/8 oz caster sugar · 8 eggs, separated
2 (230-g/8.11-oz) jars maraschino cherries

Whisk the cream with 1 tablespoon of the sugar until very thick. Cover and chill. Whisk the egg whites until they form stiff peaks. Gradually whisk in 100 g/4 oz of the remaining sugar until the meringue mixture is very thick and glossy, then fold in another 75 g/3 oz sugar and set aside. Whisk the egg yolks with the last of the sugar until very thick and light. Stir the cream, meringue and yolk mixture together.

Drain and reserve the syrup from the cherries. Coarsely chop the cherries and fold them into the ice cream. Spoon into a freezer-proof container, cover and freeze overnight.

Serve scooped into an ice bowl (page 104) or delicate glasses. The maraschino juice can be served separately in a jug. If you wish, add a little liqueur to the maraschino juice. **Serves 12**

Variation

Lychee Ice Cream Purée 1 (312-g/11-oz) can drained lychees in a liquidiser with a little of the syrup from the can. Fold the purée into the ice cream instead of the cherries.

Iced Bombe

Follow the recipe for Frozen Chestnut Pudding (opposite), omitting the chestnuts and rum. If you like, the ice cream can be left plain, or it can be flavoured with vanilla or mint essence, coffee or grated chocolate.

Pour the ice cream into a bombe mould or pudding basin and freeze until firm. When frozen, the middle of the bombe can be hollowed out and filled with grated chocolate, coffee liqueur beans, nuts or even a different flavoured ice cream. Pack some of the scooped-out ice cream on top of the filling and press down well. Re-cover and freeze again until needed. Decorate with whipped cream and preserved ginger.

Serve with Chocolate Sauce (page 123), or a simple sauce made by melting a couple of Mars Bars in a basin over hot water. **Serves 8**

Grapefruit and Mint Sorbet

1 (410-g/14½-oz) can grapefruit segments in natural juice
300 ml/½ pint water · 225 g/8 oz sugar
2–3 sprigs of mint, finely chopped · 2 egg whites

Put the grapefruit segments and juice, the water and sugar in a heavy-based saucepan. Heat gently until the sugar has dissolved. Bring to the boil and simmer for 5 minutes, then purée in a liquidiser. Cool.

Stir the mint into the cooled fruit purée and transfer it to a freezer-tray or container. Freeze until slushy. Stir well or whisk until smooth. Beat the egg whites to the soft-peak stage. Stir into the grapefruit mixture. Freeze until firm, stirring from time to time. **Serves 4 to 6**

Every time I make this I use different flowers or sometimes lemon or cucumber slices, or leaves. One of my favourites so far is wild violets.

Flower Ice Bowl

(Illustrated on page 88)

To make a flower ice bowl, you need some flowers or petals, a few sprigs of fern or a few delicate leaves; boiled, cooled water and two bowls. The bowls should be freezerproof (china, tough glass or plastic) and one should hold twice the capacity of the other.

Half fill the larger bowl with cooled boiled water, then lower in the smaller one. Put stones or ice-cubes into the smaller bowl until the rims of both are level. Float the smaller one into the centre, with about 2.5 cm/1 in of water between the bowls. Use tape to hold the bowls in position. Freeze for about 10 minutes.

Using a skewer or thin-bladed knife, poke flowers or petals, and bits of greenery in between the bowls. Replace the bowls in the freezer and leave for 24 hours. To use the ice bowl, remove the tape and the stones or ice cubes. Fill the small bowl with luke-warm water and gently twist it until it is free. Carefully lift the small bowl away from the ice. Dip the larger bowl in luke-warm water until the ice bowl can be loosened and lifted out. Replace the ice bowl in the freezer until ready to serve.

Used carefully, the bowl can be wiped out and reserved for other occasions. Smaller bowls can be made using soup or cereal bowls.

Opposite page Nanette at the fireside
Overleaf Clockwise from the top: Chocolate Roulade (page 96),
Tarte Tatin (page 93) and Frozen Chestnut Pudding (page 102)

What to Have with Coffee

Break with the tradition of inviting people over for a drink before dinner and, instead, ask them for dessert and coffee. People that you just want to see but can't manage to cope with for a dinner would probably love to come and have a spectacular dessert, some coffee and a brandy.

Opposite page Dipped Fruits (page 141), Florentines (page 113) and Nut Clusters (page 140), and Crystallised Fruits (page 141)

Impressive Dessert

1 knob of butter
32 (2 packets) sponge fingers
4–6 tablespoons Kirsch or sherry
225 g/8 oz cream cheese
600 ml/1 pint double cream
225 g/8 oz icing sugar
225 g/8 oz raspberries, pressed through a sieve
225 g/8 oz whole raspberries
DECORATION
300 ml/½ pint double cream
1 tablespoon caster sugar
1 tablespoon Kirsch (optional)

Butter a 1.75-litre/3-pint charlotte mould or pudding basin. Lightly dip the sponge fingers into the kirsch or sherry and arrange them around the sides of the mould or basin. Line the base with sponge fingers cut to fit.

Beat the cream cheese until smooth, then stir in the cream and icing sugar, and beat until very thick and smooth. Stir in the sieved raspberries. When thoroughly blended, fold in the whole raspberries. Carefully spoon the mixture into the lined mould, smooth the top and cover with any remaining sponge fingers. Cover the mould or basin with cooking foil or cling film and a small plate or saucer. Put a weight on the plate and chill overnight.

Next day, invert the mould on a serving dish (if the dessert is reluctant to come out, quickly dip the base of the mould in hot water).

Decorate no more than a couple of hours before serving. Whip the cream with the sugar and kirsch (if used) until thick. Pipe the cream mixture in vertical rows, starting at the base of the dessert, until the whole surface is completely covered. Alternatively, swirl the cream over the dessert.

The finishing touches can be as imaginative as you choose; here are some suggestions – I've tried all of these with great success – but think up some of your own if you like. Stick sugared violets and angelica leaves at regular intervals into the cream. Alternatively, decorate the top and base of the dessert with large fresh raspberries, or arrange toasted, split blanched almonds in lines all the way round. Tiny rataffia or amoretti biscuits could also be used to decorate the dessert. For a dinner party, my favourite decoration is a surround of fresh flowers (violets, pansies, freshias etc) with just one beautiful flower on the top of the dessert. Chill until ready to serve. **Serves 12**

Let Them Eat Cake

Tea parties have rather fallen out of fashion.
Now, if someone invites you for tea, it's more
likely to be a cup of tea in the kitchen and a
forage around in the biscuit tin. I remember how
nice it was when the children were at the tea-
eating stage, although it was never quite like
those teas you read about in novels: laid out on
the lawn in the summer, with cucumber
sandwiches and strawberries and cream; or winter
teas — toasting crumpets in front of a roaring fire,
and delicious slabs of fruit-filled cake.

The only time I ever become tea-party conscious
is at Christmas, when, with friends of all ages,
it's a wonderful excuse for having cakes, biscuits
and mince pies, crackers, and even a special little
Christmas tree loaded with Christmas shaped
biscuits tied on with ribbons. It's quite a good
idea to have a very large tea party on Boxing
Day, and decide to opt out of cooking dinner.

My Christmas Cake

(Illustrated on page 125)

275 g/10 oz butter · 275 g/10 oz sugar
8 eggs · 350 g/12 oz self-raising flour
½ teaspoon ground cloves · 3 teaspoons mixed spices
1.25 kg/2½ lb mixed dried fruit
225 g/8 oz chopped mixed peel
100 g/4 oz dried apricots
100 g/4 oz almonds, roughly chopped
50 g/2 oz ground almonds · 50 g/2 oz walnut pieces
grated rind and juice of 1 orange and 1 lemon
2 tablespoons brandy or rum

You could ice this but I like to leave my cake plain and tie a red ribbon round it.

Line a deep 25-cm/10-in round cake tin with greaseproof paper, then grease it thoroughly. Beat the butter and sugar together until pale and creamy. Beat in the eggs one at a time adding a teaspoon of flour occasionally to prevent the mixture from curdling. Fold in the rest of the flour and all the remaining ingredients. Mix thoroughly, then transfer the mixture to the prepared tin and smooth the top.

Bake in a cool oven (150 C, 300 F, gas 2) for 4 to 4½ hours, covering the cake with greaseproof paper after the first 2 hours. Allow the cake to cool in the tin for about 30 minutes, then turn it out on to a wire rack to cool completely. **Makes one 25-cm/10-in cake**

Katy's Christmas Cake

450 g/1 lb butter or margarine
450 g/1 lb sugar · 8 eggs, lightly beaten
450 g/1 lb self-raising flour
225 g/8 oz ground almonds
225 g/8 oz chopped mixed peel
225 g/8 oz glacé cherries, halved
1 kg/2 lb currants

Beat the butter and sugar together in a large mixing bowl until pale and creamy. Gradually add the eggs, beating the mixture continuously and adding a little flour to avoid curdling. Gently fold in the flour and ground almonds (use a metal spoon). Add the mixed peel and cherries to the cake mixture, and, finally, fold in the currants. Gently mix all the ingredients together until the fruit is evenly distributed throughout.

Turn the mixture into a lined and greased deep round 22–25-cm/9–

10-in cake tin. Make sure that the mixture is well packed in the tin, then smooth the surface with a small palette knife.

Bake in a cool oven (150 c, 300 f, gas 2) for 30 minutes, then turn the oven down to very cool (120 c, 250 f, gas $\frac{1}{2}$) and continue to cook for about a further 3 hours. To test whether the cake is done, insert a skewer in the centre, if it comes out clean the cake is cooked, if not it needs further cooking.

Remove the cake from the oven and leave to cool slightly in the tin before turning it out on to a wire rack to cool completely.

During my 'burnt boiled-egg phase', when faced with the worrying job of making a Christmas cake, Bryan's mother (Katy) gave me this simple recipe. It worked and I was so pleased with myself.

Florentines

(Illustrated on page 108)

40 g/1$\frac{1}{2}$ oz butter
125 g/4$\frac{1}{2}$ oz sugar
150 ml/$\frac{1}{4}$ pint double cream
90 g/3$\frac{1}{2}$ oz chopped mixed peel
40 g/1$\frac{1}{2}$ oz glacé cherries, chopped
40 g/1$\frac{1}{2}$ oz blanched almonds, sliced
40 g/1$\frac{1}{2}$ oz plain flour
225 g/8 oz plain chocolate, melted

Set the oven at moderate (180 c, 350 f, gas 4) and thoroughly grease several baking trays.

Melt the butter in a saucepan. Stir in the sugar and cream and bring slowly to the boil. Remove from the heat, add the fruit, nuts and flour and stir well. Drop teaspoonsfuls of the mixture on the baking trays, spacing them well apart to allow for spreading. Bake in the pre-heated oven for 10 to 12 minutes or until lightly browned at the edges. Leave on the baking trays for a few seconds, then carefully lift them off by sliding a large palette knife under each biscuit. Cool on a wire rack. If the mixture hardens before you have time to lift the florentines off the trays, return them to the oven for a minute.

Melt the chocolate in a double boiler or in a bowl placed over a pan of hot, not simmering, water. Spread the chocolate over the back of the florentines and, using a fork, mark wavy lines as a decoration. **Makes about 30**

Stollen Bread

250 ml/8 fl oz milk · 250 g/9 oz butter
100 g/4 oz caster sugar · 25 g/1 oz dried yeast
6 tablespoons tepid water
675 g/1½ lbs strong white flour
pinch each of salt, mace and nutmeg
2 eggs, lightly beaten
175 g/6 oz chopped mixed peel
100 g/4 oz sultanas · 25 g/1 oz walnuts, chopped
25 g/1 oz blanched almonds, chopped
75 g/3 oz stoned dates or apricots, chopped
4 tablespoons runny honey
4 tablespoons light soft brown sugar
pinch of cinnamon

Bring the milk to the boil, then add the butter and sugar and stir, off the heat, until melted. Allow to cool until just warm. Sprinkle the yeast over the water, adding a pinch of sugar, and stir well. Leave until frothy, then add to the milk mixture. Sift half the flour, the salt and the spices into a bowl. Make a well in the middle and add the eggs with the yeast mixture. Beat very thoroughly, either by hand or in a food mixer using a dough hook. Gradually add the remaining flour to make a soft dough, then knead it thoroughly using a dough hook or by hand (it will take about 7 to 8 minutes). The dough should be smooth and not at all sticky.

Place the dough in an oiled bowl, cover and leave in a warm place until doubled in volume. Turn the dough out on to a floured surface, add the peel, sultanas, chopped nuts and the dates or apricots. Knead well, working in the fruit, until all the ingredients are fully incorporated. Divide the dough in half and shape each portion into an oval. Place the two loaves on greased baking trays, cover with oiled polythene and leave in a warm place for about 1½ hours or until doubled in size.

Bake the loaves in a moderately hot oven (200 C, 400 F, gas 6) for 15 minutes, then reduce the oven temperature to moderate (180 C, 350 F, gas 4) and bake for a further 25 minutes. Five minutes before the end of the cooking time drizzle the honey over the loaves and sprinkle with the sugar mixed with the cinnamon. Replace the loaves in the oven to finish cooking, then cool them on a wire rack.

Serve within 24 hours, or freeze the loaves for up to 3 months.

Note: If you like add a few glacé cherries to the mixture and drizzle white glacé icing over the cooled loaves. Decorate with halved glacé cherries and strips of angelica.

Sinful Chocolate Cake

225 g/8 oz butter · 225 g/8 oz caster sugar
6 eggs, separated · 225 g/8 oz plain chocolate
150 g/5 oz ground almonds · 150 g/5 oz plain flour

Beat the butter and sugar together until pale and creamy, then add the egg yolks and beat well. Slowly add the melted chocolate and mix thoroughly. Using a metal spoon, fold in the ground almonds and flour.

In a separate bowl, whisk the egg whites until they are stiff, then fold these into the cake mixture. If this is difficult, stir a little of the white in first to soften the mixture. Pour into a well-greased 23-cm/9-in springform tin and bake in a moderate oven (180 C, 350 F, gas 4) for 60 to 70 minutes or until firm. Leave to cool in the tin before turning out.

Note: This cake also makes a great pudding, served with whipped cream, then it's even more sinful.

Whenever Edith (Dame Edith Evans) came to our home she always brought this Chocolate cake – I finally got the recipe. I've never eaten a chocolate cake I've liked better.

Kate Hepburn's Brownies

(Illustrated on page 125)

100 g/4 oz butter · 50 g/2 oz plain chocolate
225 g/8 oz sugar
$\frac{1}{4}$ teaspoon vanilla essence
75 g/3 oz self-raising flour · 2 eggs
100 g/4 oz chopped walnuts

Melt the butter and chocolate in a heavy-based saucepan over a very low heat, stirring continuously. Stir in the sugar and vanilla, then remove the pan from the heat and stir in the flour. Beat in the eggs, one at a time, and stir in the walnuts.

Line and grease a 20-cm/8-in square cake tin. Pour in the mixture and bake in a moderate oven (160 C, 325 F, gas 3) for 50 to 60 minutes or until the edges begin to shrink from the sides of the tin. Cool in the tin before cutting into squares. **Makes 16**

It is very typical of Kate that if she decides to do something she does it better than most. As a chocolate lover she only has the best chocolate recipes. She makes these chocolate brownies and naturally they are the best.

Boxing Day Carrot Cake

(Illustrated on page 125)

2 tablespoons orange juice · 1 tea bag
150 g/5 oz icing sugar · 4 eggs
350 ml/12 fl oz sunflower oil · 300 g/11 oz plain flour
1½ teaspoons baking powder
1 teaspoon each ground cinnamon and allspice
2 teaspoons grated orange rind
225 g/8 oz carrots, grated · 100 g/4 oz walnuts, chopped
icing sugar to dust the cake

Heat the orange juice, then pour it over the tea bag and leave to cool while making the cake mixture. Whisk the sugar and eggs together until pale and thick, gradually adding the oil. In a separate bowl, mix the flour, baking powder, spices and orange rind, then fold this mixture, a tablespoon at a time, into the eggs.

Fold the carrots into the cake with the orange juice and walnuts. Pour into a well-greased 20-cm/8-in cake tin and bake in a moderate oven (180 c, 350 f, gas 4) for 1½ hours, or until the cake is firm to the touch and a skewer inserted into the middle comes out clean. Cool on a wire rack, then sprinkle with icing sugar. **Makes one 20-cm/8-in cake**

Cream Cake

250 ml/8 fl oz double cream · 2 eggs
225 g/8 oz sugar
200 g/7 oz self-raising flour · ½ teaspoon salt
Topping
2 tablespoons melted butter · 2 tablespoons double cream
50 g/2 oz sugar · 50 g/2 oz blanched almonds, slivered
1 tablespoon plain flour

Whip the cream until it holds its shape. Whisk the eggs and sugar together until pale and creamy, then stir them into the cream.

Sift the flour and salt together and fold into the cake mixture, then pour it into a lined and greased 20-cm/8-in cake tin. Bake in a moderate oven (180 c, 350 f, gas 4) for 1¼ to 1½ hours. Cover the cake loosely with cooking foil if it starts to brown too quickly during cooking.

For the topping, mix the butter, cream, sugar and almonds in a small saucepan and melt these ingredients over a low heat. Stir in the flour, then spread the topping over the cake and cook for a further 10 minutes. Cool on a wire rack. **Makes one 20-cm/8-in cake**

Mince Pies

275 g/10 oz plain flour
25 g/1 oz ground almonds
175 g/6 oz butter, chilled and diced
75 g/3 oz icing sugar, sifted
grated rind of $\frac{1}{2}$ orange
1 egg yolk
3–4 tablespoons orange juice
450 g/1 lb Luxurious Mincemeat (page 144)
a little milk

Put the flour and ground almonds into a mixing bowl. Rub the butter into the flour and almonds until the mixture resembles fine breadcrumbs. Stir in the icing sugar and orange rind.

Mix the yolk with the orange juice and gradually stir it into the mixture to make a soft, but not sticky, dough. Turn out on to a floured surface. Knead gently until smooth, then wrap and chill for 20 to 30 minutes or until firm.

Roll the pastry out to 3 mm/$\frac{1}{8}$ in thick and cut out 20 to 24 circles large enough to line the base of patty tins. Cut out a further 20 to 24 smaller circles to cover the pies. Line the patty tins with the larger circles of pastry. Put a small spoonful of mincemeat in the pie cases. Brush the edges of the lids with a little cold water and place them on the pies. Press down firmly to seal the edges. Roll out any pastry trimmings and cut out stars or leaf shapes. Cut a small hole in each pie and decorate with the pastry shapes. Brush with a little milk.

Bake in a moderate oven (180 c, 350 f, gas 4) for 15 to 20 minutes until golden brown. Sprinkle with icing sugar and allow to cool in the tins for 5 minutes before transferring to a cooling rack. Store in an airtight tin. Serve hot or cold, with Brandy Butter (below). **Makes 20 to 24**

Brandy Butter

100 g/4 oz unsalted butter
100 g/4 oz icing sugar, sifted
4 tablespoons brandy

Cream the butter with the sugar until smooth and light, then beat in the brandy. Pile into a small dish to serve. **Serves 6**

Apricot Cookies

100 g/4 oz butter or margarine
100 g/4 oz granulated sugar
50 g/2 oz light brown sugar
1 egg
1 teaspoon vanilla essence
150 g/5 oz plain flour
$\frac{1}{2}$ teaspoon salt
$\frac{1}{2}$ teaspoon bicarbonate of soda
175 g/6 oz dried apricots, coarsely chopped

Cream together the butter, sugars, egg and vanilla essence until smooth. Gradually work in the flour, salt and bicarbonate of soda and mix thoroughly. Add the apricots and stir well.

Put teaspoonfuls of the mixture about 5 cm/2 in apart on greased baking trays and bake in a moderately hot oven (190 c, 375 f, gas 5) for 10 minutes, or until the cookies are evenly golden. Allow to cool slightly on the baking trays before transferring to a wire rack. **Makes about 26**

Ginger Thins

225 g/8 oz plain flour
2 teaspoons ground ginger
100 g/4 oz butter, diced
175 g/6 oz light soft brown sugar
1 egg, beaten

Grease several baking trays. Sift the flour and ginger into a mixing bowl. Add the butter and rub it in until the mixture resembles fine breadcrumbs. Stir in the sugar and enough of the beaten egg to make a stiff dough. Turn on to a floured surface and knead quickly until smooth. Shape into a 2.5-cm/1-in diameter roll.

Wrap in cooking foil or cling film and place in the deep freeze until almost frozen. Using a very sharp knife, cut the mixture into thin slices. Place well apart on the prepared baking trays and bake in a moderately hot oven (190 c, 375 f, gas 5) for 5 to 7 minutes, or until golden. Cool the thins on the baking trays for a few minutes, then transfer them to a wire rack to cool completely. **Makes about 30**

Peanut Cookies

100 g/4 oz butter
175 g/6 oz sugar
100 g/4 oz smooth peanut butter
1 egg, lightly beaten
2 teaspoons vanilla essence
3 tablespoons milk
275 g/10 oz plain flour
$\frac{1}{2}$ teaspoon salt
$\frac{1}{2}$ teaspoon baking powder

Beat the butter and sugar together until pale and creamy. Add the peanut butter, beating until smooth and creamy. Slowly beat in the egg, vanilla essence and milk, then continue beating until thoroughly combined. Fold in the flour, salt and baking powder, and chill.

Divide the mixture in half. Roll out each piece to give a rectangle measuring 15 × 25 cm/6 × 10 in. Carefully roll up one sheet of the dough (as you would a Swiss roll) and wrap it in cling film. Repeat with the other sheet of dough. Chill for an hour, or until the mixture is firm. When firm, unwrap the rolls and gently reshape them if they have flattened slightly underneath, then cut them into thin slices and place these on greased baking trays.

Bake in a moderately hot oven (190 c, 375 f, gas 5) for 8 to 10 minutes, or until lightly browned. Cool on a wire rack; the cookies should be swirled like a Swiss roll. **Makes about 24**

Sarah's Chocolate Chip Cookies

(Illustrated on page 145)

225 g/8 oz butter
175 g/6 oz soft brown sugar
175 g/6 oz caster sugar
2 eggs, beaten
1 teaspoon vanilla essence
250 g/9 oz self-raising flour
1 teaspoon baking powder
1 teaspoon bicarbonate of soda
1 teaspoon salt
3 (115-g/4-oz) packets chocolate chips

Cream the butter and sugars together until soft. Gradually add the eggs beating continuously, then stir in the vanilla essence. Gently stir in the flour, baking powder, bicarbonate of soda and salt, and mix thoroughly. Stir in the chocolate chips, one packet at a time.

Spoon teaspoonfuls of the mixture on to greased baking trays, keeping them quite small and spaced well apart because the mixture will spread during cooking. Bake in a moderate oven (180 c, 350 F, gas 4) for 10 to 12 minutes, or until the cookies are golden brown. Allow them to cool slightly on the baking trays before transferring to a wire rack to cool completely. **Makes about 40**

Sarah, my daughter, is a superb cook. She is inventive, and there are many things that I have copied from her. This is her recipe for Chocolate Chip Cookies — I've never found a better one. Make them for yourself or to give away (quickly, because once tried you tend to throw all thoughts of diet away and give in to becoming an addict).

Children's Boxing Day Tea Party

As a child I loved Christmas. My family were often short of money but they never lacked the ability to enjoy themselves. Christmas would see all the relatives and friends crammed into my grandmother's small house. We children had a great time squabbling over the decoration of the tree, writing and rewriting letters to be posted up the chimney to Father Christmas, heaving hints and whisperings about presents we hoped to receive. There was holly over the pictures, mistletoe to be giggled under, a once-a-year turkey dinner, carols and sing-songs. We were allowed to stay up late, then we were too excited to sleep and would wake early to pounce upon bulging stockings, pretending to believe in Father Christmas long after the truth was known because it was all part of the mystery of Christmas.

I was lucky: my memories are happy ones and when I had children of my own I wanted their memories to be happy too. The following is an idea for a children's Christmas tea party which, hopefully, they will remember.

Loaf Box Sandwiches

(Illustrated on pages 126/127)

I prefer wholemeal bread for nearly everything but the choice is yours.

1 large cottage loaf
1 large loaf of brown bread to make sandwiches
175 g/6 oz softened butter
FILLING SUGGESTIONS
marmite and lettuce
hard-boiled egg, mashed with a little mayonnaise
cooked kippers, cooled, boned and mixed with a little cream,
lemon juice and pepper
cream cheese mixed with chopped stoned dates and mashed
bananas

Using a long, sharp bread knife, cut the top off the cottage loaf and carefully hollow it out (the inside can be used for breadcrumbs). Thinly slice and butter the loaf for sandwiches. Use the chosen fillings to sandwich the buttered bread. Trim off the crusts, then cut each sandwich into tiny squares or thin fingers.

Neatly pack them into the hollowed-out loaf, replace the lid and tie with ribbon, just like a parcel. The sandwiches will keep very fresh and moist for up to 2 hours, or the loaf can be wrapped in cling film and chilled for up to 5 hours.

Simple Tuna Dip

(Illustrated on pages 126/127)

175 g/6 oz cream cheese
1 (198-g/7-oz) can tuna fish, drained and flaked
3 tablespoons mayonnaise
2 tablespoons chopped celery
1 tablespoon lemon juice
salt and pepper

Mix all the ingredients together. Press the dip into tiny dishes (those which are used for serving individual portions of butter) and place each one on a large plate.

Arrange a selection of crackers, celery and carrot strips, and crisps all around the dip. This way you will avoid any spills. **Serves 8**

Chocolate Sauce for Ice Cream

100 g/4 oz chocolate · 50 g/2 oz butter
2 tablespoons golden syrup
6 tablespoons double cream

Melt the chocolate in a basin over a saucepan of hot, not simmering, water. Add the butter and syrup and stir until melted. Remove from the heat and stir in the cream. Serve hot. **Makes about 300 ml/½ pint.**

Both my daughters were brought up to think of sweets and ice creams as a treat and when on a trip to Hollywood I told Sarah (then five years old) that I would take her to an amazing ice cream parlour where there were forty flavours to choose from. She couldn't wait and couldn't stop talking about it. When we finally got there she sat and stared at the enormous menu. I explained all the flavours and all the different toppings and sauces; she sat for ages pondering the great decision and finally said 'I'll have vanilla'. Children do not get their reputation for being unpredictable for nothing! I, on the other hand, was the one who had the largest, gooiest concoction with everything on top and, of course, I was the one who felt sick.

Gingerbread Men

(Illustrated on pages 126/127)

225 g/8 oz plain flour · pinch of salt
2 teaspoons ground ginger · 150 g/5 oz butter
1 egg, separated · 2 tablespoons black treacle
25 g/1 oz sugar *plus* 15 g/½ oz sugar to glaze
DECORATION
a few currants · stiff glacé icing (optional)

Sift the dry ingredients into a mixing bowl and rub in the butter until the mixture resembles fine breadcrumbs. Add the egg yolk, black treacle and sugar, mix thoroughly then knead lightly and roll out on a floured surface to 5 mm/¼ in thick. Cut out shapes of gingerbread men – or even gingerbread families and place the biscuits on greased baking trays. Brush with egg white, sprinkle with sugar and use the currants to decorate the biscuits. Bake in a moderate oven (180 C, 350 F, gas 4) for 12 to 15 minutes, until golden. Cool slightly on the baking trays, then transfer to a wire rack. Decorate with icing. **Makes about 18**
Note: You can decorate the gingerbread men to make Father Christmas biscuits – add red icing hats and white icing beards.

Mixed-up Cake

(Illustrated on pages 126/127)

3 eggs · 175 g/6 oz caster sugar
225 g/8 oz butter, thoroughly softened
200 g/7 oz plain flour · ½ teaspoon salt
2½ teaspoons baking powder
1 teaspoon vanilla essence · 200 ml/7 fl oz milk
50 g/2 oz plain chocolate, melted
50 g/2 oz cocoa powder

Whisk the eggs and sugar together until pale and thick enough to hold the trace of the whisk for 5 seconds. In another bowl, beat the butter until very pale and soft (it should be similar to whipped cream) then add spoonfuls of the butter to the egg mixture and beat each addition in thoroughly. Fold in the flour, salt, baking powder and vanilla. Gradually stir in the milk, then set half the mixture aside and fold in the melted chocolate and cocoa powder.

Line and grease a 20-cm/8-in deep cake tin. Put heaped tablespoons of each mixture into the tin, leaving the two colours quite separate. Bake in a moderate oven (180 C, 350 F, gas 4) for 50 minutes. Allow to cool slightly before turning out on to a wire rack to cool completely.

Either sift icing sugar over the cake or swirl the Cream Cheese Frosting over it, if you like. **Makes one 20-cm/8-in cake.**

Cream Cheese Frosting: Cream 100 g/4 oz cream cheese with 50 g/2 oz butter, 2 teaspoons double cream and 275 g/10 oz sifted icing sugar. Beat well until thoroughly mixed.

Frozen Chocolate Bananas

(Illustrated overleaf)

Melt 450 g/1 lb plain chocolate in a basin over a saucepan of hot water. Dip ten peeled bananas in the chocolate to coat them completely and stick a skewer in each one. Freeze on a baking tray covered with cling film for at least one hour, but not more than 4 or 5 hours. **Makes 10**

Opposite page My Christmas Cake (page 112) with Boxing Day Carrot Cake (page 116), Kate Hepburn's Brownies (page 115) and a selection of cookies
Overleaf Children's Boxing Day Tea Party

Drinks and Things to Have with Them

We have become a nation of wine drinkers, and that has simplified what to give people who don't care for spirits.

Perhaps at Christmas you might want to produce something that is more festive in origin. If you are having friends in just for drinks, then it's nice to offer something to eat as well but if the people are staying to dinner, then make the offering non-filling: just something to set their tastebuds going. Otherwise (as we often say to children) they won't be able to eat their dinner up. Always try and have some prepared raw vegetables for the dieters, or those who know there is something delicious to come.

Opposite page Stilton Savouries (page 131), Tuna and Horseradish Dip (page 132) and Brie in Pastry (page 133) with Mulled Wine (page 130) and Peach Juice and Champagne (131)

Mulled Wine

(Illustrated on page 128)

1 orange
1 lemon
2 bottles red wine
2 long cinnamon sticks (about 7.5 cm/3 in)
4 cloves
100 g/4 oz sugar
6 tablespoons water
pinch of mixed spice

Pare all the rind from both the orange and the lemon, taking care not to include any of the pith. Place the fruit rinds in a saucepan with the wine and all the remaining ingredients, then simmer gently for 5 minutes. **Serves 12**

Café Brûlot

2 teaspoons sugar
1 small cinnamon stick
grated rind of 1 small orange
$\frac{1}{4}$ teaspoon ground cloves
6 tablespoons cognac, warmed
900 ml/1$\frac{1}{2}$ pints freshly made strong coffee
a little lightly whipped cream (optional)

Mix all the ingredients (except the cream) in a warmed bowl and serve in heatproof glasses. Top each serving with a little cream if you like. **Serves 6**

Christmas Grog

750 ml/1$\frac{1}{4}$ pints boiling water
2 orange pekoe tea bags
150 ml/$\frac{1}{4}$ pint rum
2 tablespoons brown sugar
pinch of cinnamon

Pour the boiling water over the tea bags and set aside to cool. Strain the tea into a saucepan and add all the remaining ingredients. Heat through and serve in mugs. **Serves 6**

Peach Juice and Champagne

(or Bucks Fizz Gone to Heaven)

(Illustrated on page 128)

Mix together equal quantities of chilled champagne and peach juice. (Bottles of peach juice can be bought in delicatessen and specialist shops.) For real luxury add diced fresh peaches. Experiment with other exotic fruit juices, if you like, instead of the peach juice.

Stilton Savouries

(Illustrated on page 128)

100 g/4 oz plain flour
100 g/4 oz unsalted butter, chilled and cubed
100 g/4 oz Stilton cheese, crumbled
beaten egg to glaze
75 g/3 oz walnuts, chopped

Put the flour, butter and Stilton in a food processor and mix briefly to give a smooth dough. Alternatively, knead all the ingredients together by hand. Wrap and chill for 1 hour or until firm.

Lightly grease several baking trays. Roll out the dough to 5 cm/$\frac{1}{4}$ in thick. Cut into 5-cm/2-in squares, then cut the squares in half diagonally to make triangles. Place on the baking sheets and chill for 10 minutes. Brush with beaten egg and sprinkle with chopped walnuts. Bake in a moderately hot oven (190 C, 375 F, gas 5) for 5 to 7 minutes, or until golden. Transfer to a wire rack to cool. These nibbles can be served hot or warm, or they can be made in advance and briefly reheated before serving or they can be frozen. **Makes about 30**

Crispy Potato Skins

Brush a baking tin with sunflower oil, then add thin strips of scrubbed and dried potato peelings and sprinkle a little oil over them. Arrange the pieces of skin in one layer and sprinkle with coarse sea salt. Bake in a moderately hot oven (190 C, 375 F, gas 5), turning once or twice, until brown and crisp – about 20 minutes.

These go particularly well with a dip made from soured cream and chopped fresh chives.

Tuna and Horseradish Dip

(Illustrated on page 128)

1 (200-g/7-oz) can tuna, drained
2 teaspoons horseradish sauce
1 tablespoon mayonnaise
2 teaspoons lemon juice
freshly ground black papper

Place all the ingredients in a liquidiser and blend together until smooth. Chill before serving, with a selection of sliced vegetables, apples and plain crackers. **Serves 6**

Cheese Nut Ball with Fruit

50 g/2 oz Cheddar cheese, grated
100 g/4 oz Stilton cheese, crumbled
450 g/1 lb cream cheese
2 tablespoons soured cream
2 teaspoons red wine
1 tablespoon chopped parsley
275 g/10 oz mixed nuts, chopped (try walnuts or cashews)

Blend the cheeses together with the soured cream and red wine. Stir in the chopped parsley, then chill until firm.

Sprinkle the nuts on to a wooden board, or clean surface, and turn out the cheese mixture on top. Carefully roll the cheese into a ball, coating it evenly in the nuts.

Chill the cheese ball for at least 30 minutes, or until required, then serve with sliced apples, celery and crackers. **Serves 12**

Note: Odds and ends of cheese, leftover from a cheeseboard, can be used in this cheese ball.

Brie in Pastry

(Illustrated on page 128)

450 g/1 lb prepared phyllo dough
50 g/2 oz butter, melted
225 g/8 oz firm Brie, thoroughly chilled
beaten egg to glaze

Keep any extra sheets of phyllo pastry covered in cling film as you work. Cut the pastry into 5-cm/2-in wide strips, measuring about 15 cm/6 in. in length. Brush them with melted butter. Cut the cheese into 1-cm/$\frac{1}{2}$-in dice and place one piece at one end of each strip of pastry. Fold the pastry over and over to enclose the cheese in a triangle shape completely, and tuck the end in neatly.

Place on greased baking trays and chill for 15 minutes. Brush the pastry with beaten egg and bake in a hot oven (220 C, 425 F, gas 7) for 5 to 7 minutes, until puffed and golden. Serve warm. **Makes 30**

Note: A quick alternative is to prepare a whole, small Camembert in pastry. Scrape off the rind, then chill the cheese very thoroughly in a freezer: it should be almost frozen before it is wrapped and baked as above.

Spinach Balls

100 g/4 oz frozen chopped spinach, thawed
50 g/2 oz Parmesan cheese, grated
50 g/2 oz butter
150 ml/$\frac{1}{4}$ pint milk and water (half and half, mixed)
75 g/3 oz plain flour · pinch of salt
2 eggs, beaten

Thoroughly drain the spinach and purée it with the cheese. Place the butter and liquid in a saucepan and heat slowly until the butter melts. Stir in the spinach purée, bring rapidly to the boil, then immediately stir in all the flour and salt. Stir quickly so that the mixture forms a smooth ball of paste which leaves the sides of the pan clean. Allow to cool slightly, then beat in the eggs until smooth and glossy.

Drop tiny, neat spoonfuls of the mixture on to greased baking trays and bake in a moderately hot oven (200 C, 400 F, gas 6) for 15 to 20 minutes until puffed and golden. Cool on a wire rack. **Makes 40**

Children's Honey Snack

*This is useful for children when you have friends in for drinks. Give
the children a glass of sparkling spring water with a slice of lemon
and a bowlful of this to keep them happy.*

75 g/3 oz desiccated coconut
75 g/3 oz jumbo oats
75 g/3 oz crunchy breakfast cereal
150 g/5 oz mixed nuts
3 tablespoons sunflower oil
1 tablespoon brown sugar
2–3 tablespoons honey

Mix all the ingredients together and spread the mixture out on a baking
tray. Bake in a moderate oven (180 C, 350 F, gas 4) for about 30 minutes,
or until the snack is crisp and brown. Turn the mixture occasionally
during cooking and again at the end of the cooking time. Allow to cool
on the tin before storing in an airtight container.

Popcorn with Nuts

65 g/2½ oz butter · 150 g/5 oz popping corn
25 g/1 oz hazelnuts · 25 g/1 oz brazil nuts
25 g/1 oz almonds · 25 g/1 oz walnuts
CARAMEL
425 g/15 oz butter · 275 g/10 oz sugar

For this you will need a large saucepan with a tight-fitting lid. Melt the
butter in the saucepan and heat it until a haze can be seen above the fat.
Add the popcorn, immediately reduce the heat to low and put the lid on
the pan. Shake the pan vigorously until all the popping has ceased.
Remove from the heat and add the nuts.

In another pan, mix the butter and sugar for the caramel until the
sugar has dissolved, then simmer until the mixture turns golden. Pour
the caramel over the popcorn and nut mixture and stir well.

Variation

Savoury Popcorn: Make a batch of popcorn (cook the corn in hot
sunflower oil in a large covered saucepan) and turn it into a large bowl.
Sprinkle with salt and offer the corn with drinks.

Presents Good Enough to Eat

An American friend, Barbara Nichols, gave me the most thoughtful Christmas present one year. A beautiful box with layer upon layer of home-made cookies. The box was so pretty that it went straight on the table as it was and the cookies were superb.

These are her recipes for this very original gift, as well as some others that you may enjoy making and giving.

Christmas Cookies

6 eggs
450 g/1 oz dark soft brown sugar
225 g/8 oz plain flour
scant 1 tablespoon ground cinnamon
2 teaspoons ground allspice
225 g/8 oz plain chocolate, grated
225 g/8 oz walnuts, broken
ICING
225 g/8 oz icing sugar
a few drops of lemon juice

Separate two of the eggs and reserve the whites, then beat the yolks with the whole eggs. Gradually mix in the sugar, flour and spices until smooth. Stir in the chocolate and nuts and spread this mixture over a greased and floured 23 × 33-cm/9 × 13-in Swiss roll tin. Bake in a moderate oven (180 c, 350 f, gas 4) for about 25 to 35 minutes. Cool in the tin, then cut into squares.

To make the icing, sift the icing sugar into a bowl, then gradually beat it into the reserved egg whites until smooth. Stir in the lemon juice. Pipe the icing on the cookies in the shape of initials, names or any decoration of your own choice. **Makes about 30**

Date and Almond Chews

225 g/8 oz whole blanched almonds
450 g/1 lb stoned dates, chopped
225 g/8 oz caster sugar
2 egg whites
1 teaspoon vanilla essence
15 glacé cherries, halved

In a large mixing bowl, combine the almonds, dates, sugar, egg whites and vanilla essence. Stir thoroughly until the mixture becomes sticky, then chill for an hour.

Using your hands, shape the mixture into small cones and place them on greased baking trays. Top each with half a cherry and bake in a moderate oven (180 c, 350 f, gas 4) for 20 minutes or until the almonds are slightly brown. Allow the chews to cool on the baking sheet before transferring them to a wire rack. **Makes about 30**

Almond Cookies

3 egg whites
225 g/8 oz caster sugar
350 g/12 oz ground almonds
almond slivers for decoration

Whisk the egg whites until stiff. Gradually add the sugar and ground almonds and mix thoroughly until the mixture is stiff. Using your hands, shape the mixture into a large ball.

Either spoon small amounts of the mixture on to a greased baking tray or shape small portions into balls. Decorate with slivered almonds and bake in a moderate oven (180 c, 350 f, gas 4) for 10 to 12 minutes, or until golden brown. Cool on a wire rack. **Makes about 34**

Butter Cookies

450 g/1 lb butter
225 g/8 oz caster sugar
2 eggs, separated
grated rind and juice of $\frac{1}{2}$ lemon
675 g/1$\frac{1}{2}$ lb plain flour
1 teaspoon baking powder
TOPPING
225 g/8 oz blanched almonds, chopped
a little sugar
ground cinnamon

Beat the butter and sugar together until pale and creamy. Gradually add the egg yolks, beating continuously until the mixture is creamy. Fold in the lemon rind and juice, the flour and baking powder. Mix thoroughly, then cover and chill the dough for about 2 hours.

Divide the dough into two or three portions, knead lightly into balls, then roll out on a lightly floured surface. Use a 5-cm/2-in cutter to cut out the cookies and place them on greased baking trays. Brush with the egg whites and sprinkle with chopped almonds, sugar and a little cinnamon. Bake in a moderate oven (180 c, 350 f, gas 4) for 12 to 15 minutes, or until just beginning to brown. Cool on a wire rack. **Makes 45**

Christmas Tree Cookies

100 g/4 oz margarine · 50 g/2 oz lard
225 g/8 oz sugar · 2 eggs, lightly beaten
1 teaspoon vanilla essence
350 g/12 oz plain flour
3 teaspoons baking powder

Cream the margarine, lard and sugar together very thoroughly. Slowly add the eggs and beat until the mixture is really creamy. Add the vanilla essence and stir in the flour and baking powder until well mixed. Wrap in cling film and chill for approximately 2 hours.

Divide the mixture into six portions and roll each one out on a lightly floured surface. Use Christmas biscuit cutters to cut out the cookies; for example: stars, crosses, tree shapes or a variety of animals. Place on greased baking trays and use a skewer to make a small hole near the top of each shape. Bake in a moderate oven (180 c, 350 f, gas 4) for 10 minutes or until just lightly coloured. Cool on a wire rack.

Makes about 70 small cookies

Note: Decorate the cookies yourself or better still get your children to decorate them with glacé icing, nuts and cherries or chocolate. Thread ribbon through the holes to hang the cookies on the tree.

Meringue Initials

(Illustrated on pages 126/127)

4 egg whites · 225 g/8 oz caster sugar
a little extra caster sugar

Whisk the egg whites until they are very stiff, then gradually add the sugar whisking continuously until it has all been added.

Put the meringue into an icing bag fitted with a large star nozzle and pipe the initials on oiled baking trays. Sprinkle with caster sugar and dry out the meringues in a very cool oven (120 c, 250 f, gas $\frac{1}{2}$) for $1\frac{1}{2}$ to 2 hours or until the meringues are crisp and dry. Remove from the oven and cool on a wire rack. Serve in a basket for a children's party, so that the children can pick out their own initials, or give them as a gift. **Makes about 30.**

When dining with my friend Bridget, she served these initials with crème brûlée.

Gingerbread Hearts and Edible Labels for Gifts

(Illustrated on page 145)

Use the dough mixture for Ginger Thins (page 118). When the mixture is thoroughly chilled, roll it out to 5 mm/$\frac{1}{4}$ in thick on a floured surface. Cut out heart shapes using a biscuit cutter (or draw a heart shape on stiff cardboard and cut round this) or cut out parcel tag shapes. Make a small hole in the top of each heart (it should be large enough to thread a ribbon through). Make similar holes in the top or all round the edges of the labels. Transfer the biscuits to greased baking trays and chill them for 10 minutes.

Bake in a moderate oven (180 c, 350 f, gas 4) for 15 to 20 minutes, or until golden brown. Allow the biscuits to cool slightly on the tins, then transfer them to a wire rack to cool completely.

When cold, thread ribbons through the holes in the top of the hearts and round the labels (as shown in the picture) and use glacé or royal icing to pipe a name on each heart, or a message on each label.

When the ribbons are removed, the biscuits can be eaten.

Fudge

(Illustrated on page 145)

175 ml/6 fl oz milk
50 g/2 oz plain chocolate
450 g/1 lb sugar
1 tablespoon golden syrup
2 tablespoons melted butter
50 g/2 oz hazelnuts, chopped

In a saucepan, mix the milk, chocolate, sugar and syrup. Stir over low heat until dissolved and well blended, then bring to the boil and boil until the mixture reaches the soft ball stage: 115–120 c/235–245 f on a sugar thermometer. When you place the thermometer in the mixture make sure that it does not rest on the base of the pan; hold it suspended in the fudge.

Remove the pan from the heat and stir in the melted butter. Add the hazelnuts and beat the mixture thoroughly until thick. Finally, stir in the chopped hazelnuts and pour the mixture into a greased shallow tin. Leave until half set, then cut the fudge into pieces and set aside until firm.
Makes about 50 pieces

Truffles

(Illustrated on page 145)

350 g/12 oz digestive biscuits, crushed
100 g/4 oz walnuts, chopped
2 tablespoons golden syrup
100 ml/4 fl oz rum or brandy
7–8 tablespoons cocoa powder, sifted
100 g/4 oz caster sugar

Thoroughly mix the crushed biscuits, nuts, syrup, rum or brandy, 2 tablespoons of the cocoa powder and the caster sugar in a bowl. Shape the biscuit mixture into small, walnut-sized balls and roll each one in the remaining cocoa powder. Chill thoroughly before serving. **Makes about 60**

Nut Clusters

(Illustrated on page 108)

450 g/1 lb dark plain dessert chocolate
175 g/6 oz mixed nuts, chopped (try almonds, hazelnuts and walnuts)
25 g/1 oz crystallised ginger, chopped
50 g/2 oz candied peel, chopped

Melt half the chocolate in a bowl over a pan of hot water. Stir in the nuts, ginger and peel. Line a baking tray with waxed or non-stick baking paper. Put heaped teaspoonfuls of the mixture on the paper and leave in a cool place to set overnight. Next day, melt the remaining chocolate in the same way and, using two forks, quickly dip the nut clusters into the chocolate to coat them evenly. Leave to set on the paper, as before. **Makes about 24**

Note: If you like you can simply mix the ingredients into all the melted chocolate and allow the spoonfuls of mixture to set.

Dipped Fruits

(Illustrated on page 108)

Californian or New Zealand strawberries are now available at Christmas time. Melt plain dessert chocolate in a bowl over a pan of hot water, stir gently until smooth and dip the strawberries into the chocolate so that they are half cooked. Lay them on a baking tray lined with non-stick baking paper and leave in a cool place until set. If strawberries are out of the question, try dipping cherries or mandarin segments. For those who like marzipan, shape pieces into acorns and dip them into the chocolate.

Crystallised Fruits

(Illustrated on page 108)

It is important to choose firm ripe fruit. Suitable fruits are pineapple slices (peeled and cored), stoned and halved apricots or plums, whole small pears, peeled or whole mandarins. If you are going to cook small fruits whole, it is best to prick them well so the sugar syrup can be absorbed easily. Soft fruits (such as berries) are not suitable. The prepared fruit should be weighed and put into a large, heavy-based saucepan (not aluminium). Pour in 300 ml/$\frac{1}{2}$ pint of water to every 450 g/1 lb of fruit. Cover and simmer gently until the fruit softens – about 15 minutes for pineapple slices or 2 to 3 minutes for softer fruits. Carefully lift out the fruit and measure the liquid in the pan. Pour the liquid back into the pan and add 125 g/$4\frac{1}{2}$ oz powdered glucose and 50 g/2 oz of granulated sugar to every 300 ml/$\frac{1}{2}$ pint of liquid. Stir over low heat until the sugar and glucose dissolves. Bring to the boil and simmer for one minute. Remove from the heat and add the fruit. Cover with a piece of damp greaseproof paper and leave overnight. Next day, remove the fruit from the pan. As before, measure the syrup and this time add 50 g/2 oz sugar to every 300 ml/$\frac{1}{2}$ pint of liquid. Put the liquid and the sugar into the pan, dissolve and simmer as before. Add the fruit, off the heat, cover the pan and leave overnight. Do this every day for the next five days, then increase the sugar to 75 g/3 oz and repeat as before, this time leaving the fruit undisturbed for 48 hours. Repeat this last process once more. When the final 48 hours is up, drain the fruit from any syrup that is left and put it on a cooling rack to dry. This can be done in an airing cupboard (set the rack over a baking tray to catch any drips) or in any other place that is warm and dry. When the fruit feels dry (not sticky) to touch it's ready. Store in airtight containers, lined with greaseproof or waxed paper and keep in a cool, dry place.

Home-made Chutney

(Illustrated on page 145)

1.5 kg/3½ lb tomatoes, peeled and chopped
675 g/1½ lb cooking apples, peeled, cored and chopped
675 g/1½ lb dessert apples, peeled, cored and chopped
675 g/1½ lb onions, peeled and chopped
350 g/12 oz red peppers, chopped
350 g/12 oz green peppers, chopped
450 g/1 lb stoned raisins
100 g/4 oz preserved ginger, chopped
4 teaspoons salt
4 teaspoons pickling spices, tied in a muslin bag
1.15 litres/2 pints cider vinegar
1 kg/2 lb soft light brown sugar

Put the prepared tomatoes, apples, onions, peppers, raisins and ginger in a large saucepan. Stir in the salt, bag of spices, and 900 ml/1½ pints of the vinegar. Stir well. Bring to the boil, stirring from time to time, then simmer, stirring occasionally, for 1½ hours or until the vegetables are soft. Add the remaining vinegar and the sugar. Stir over low heat until the sugar has dissolved. Boil rapidly until the mixture is very thick. Stir, then pour into clean, sterilised jars. Cover tightly when cool and label.
Makes about 2.75 kg/6 lb

Dried Apricot and Ginger Preserve

(Illustrated on page 145)

675 g/1½ lb dried apricots
1 litre/1¾ pints water
675 g/1½ lb sugar
juice of ½ lemon
50 g/2 oz crystallised ginger, chopped
65 g/2½ oz blanched almonds, cut in slivers

Soak the apricots in water for 8 hours or overnight. Drain. Put into a large pan with the water and simmer gently for an hour or until very soft.

Add the sugar, lemon juice and ginger, then stir frequently, without boiling, until the sugar has dissolved. Stir in the almonds, raise the heat and boil rapidly, stirring from time to time, until setting point is reached. To test for setting, spoon a little of the preserve on to a clean, cold saucer and leave it for a minute. If setting point is reached the preserve should have formed a skin which will wrinkle when pushed with your finger.

Cool until lukewarm, then spoon into clean and dry sterilized jars. When cold, seal, cover and label. **Makes about 2.75 kg/6 lbs**

Special Whisky Preserve

(Illustrated on page 85)

1 kg/2 lb oranges
450 g/1 lb mixture of grapefruit and lemons
2 cloves
3 litres/5 pints water
2.75 kg/6 lb preserving sugar, warmed
1 teaspoon black treacle
150 ml/$\frac{1}{4}$ pint whisky

Wash the fruit. Using a sharp vegetable peeler, thinly peel the oranges and grapefruit. Shred the rind and put it in a preserving pan or large heavy-based saucepan. Remove and reserve the pith from the oranges and grapefruit and put on one side. Segment the prepared fruit and place in the pan.

Peel the lemons, and mix the rind with the reserved grapefruit and orange pith. Squeeze all the juice from the lemons, then pour it into the pan. Tie the reserved pith, lemon rind, any pips and leftover bits of fruit in a muslin bag with the cloves. Put in the pan with the water. Simmer the mixture, uncovered, for 2 hours or until half the liquid has evaporated, and the rind is soft. Stir in the warmed sugar, and the treacle. Stir over low heat until dissolved. Bring to a boil and boil rapidly until setting point is reached. (See Dried Apricot and Ginger Preserve, opposite, for instructions for testing for setting.) Add the whisky, stir and boil for another 5 minutes. Remove from the heat and remove the muslin bag, carefully squeezing to extract the juices. Allow to cool, then pour into clean sterilized dry jars. Cover tightly and label.
Makes 2.75 kg/6 lb

Luxurious Mincemeat

450 g/1 lb stoned raisins
450 g/1 lb currants
450 g/1 lb sultanas
225 g/8 oz crystallised fruits *or* chopped mixed peel
175 g/6 oz blanched almonds
75 g/3 oz walnuts
175 g/6 oz glacé cherries
6 cooking apples
450 g/1 lb dark soft brown sugar
generous pinch of salt
grated rind and juice of 2 lemons
1 teaspoon ground ginger
$1\frac{1}{2}$ teaspoons cinnamon
1 teaspoon nutmeg
$\frac{1}{2}$ teaspoon ground cloves
225 g/8 oz butter, melted
4 large bananas, diced
300 ml/$\frac{1}{2}$ pint brandy

Wash and thoroughly dry the raisins, currants and sultanas. Finely chop the crystallised fruit (if used). Shred the almonds, and chop the walnuts and cherries. Wash, core and grate the apples with their peel. Mix all these ingredients in a large mixing bowl with the sugar, salt, lemon rind and juice and the four spices. Pour a quarter of the butter into a non-stick frying pan and, when hot, briefly stir-fry the bananas until they are golden. Add the bananas to the fruit with the remaining butter. Mix well, then stir in the brandy. Store in covered jars for not more than 3 weeks. **Makes about 4 kg/9 lb**

Opposite page A selection of edible gifts: Home-made Chutney, Dried Apricot and Ginger Preserve and Special Whisky Preserve (all on pages 142/143); Fudge (page 139) and Truffles (page 140)
Overleaf A new year's eve party menu: Coulibiac, Cabbage Filled with Dip and Tremendous Trifle (pages 150–152)

Happy Endings

I have never liked large new year's eve
celebrations with lots of noise and shouting,
when you suddenly find yourself linking arms
with a total stranger to sing Auld Lang Syne.
I like to see the old year out with best friends
and loved ones around me — so I have arranged a
new year's eve menu that will work equally well
for my type of party or for a large celebration.
Here are some ideas that you can adapt or
which, at the very least, will set you thinking.

Menu

Coulibiac

Cabbage Filled with Dip

Big Green Salad

Tremendous Trifle

Opposite page A Victorian Salmon Soufflé (page 70) and Savoury
Stuffed Pears (page 20)

Coulibiac

(Illustrated on pages 146/147)

This Russian fish pie is traditionally served at weddings and celebration feasts. Fresh salmon tastes best, but it can be replaced with canned salmon or cooked chicken.

50 g/2 oz butter
2 large onions, finely chopped
350 g/12 oz mushrooms, sliced
175 g/6 oz long-grain rice
2 tablespoons chopped parsley or chives
450 g/1 lb cooked fresh salmon
3 hard-boiled eggs, sliced
2 tablespoons lemon juice · salt and pepper
450 g/1 lb puff pastry (you can use a 454-g/1-lb packet frozen
pastry, thawed, or your own home-made)
beaten egg to glaze

Melt the butter in a frying pan, add the onions and cook slowly until soft. Add the mushrooms and stir-fry over low heat for 2 minutes. Remove from the heat and allow to cool. Meanwhile, cook the rice in boiling salted water until tender. Rinse and drain thoroughly, then add to the onion mixture with the parsley or chives.

Remove the skin and bones from the salmon and flake the fish. Add to the onion and rice mixture. Slice the hard-boiled eggs and add to the filling with the lemon juice and seasoning. Gently mix all the ingredients together.

Roll out the pastry 5 mm/$\frac{1}{4}$ in thick to give a rectangle measuring about 42.5 × 25 cm/17 × 10 in. Trim the edges. (Reserve the trimmings and use them for the decoration.) Brush the pastry with a little beaten egg. Spoon the salmon mixture on to the pastry, moulding it into a neat mound with your hands. Fold the long edges of the pastry up over the filling, to meet and overlap in the middle. Brush the pastry with egg between the overlap and fold the ends in to seal the coulibiac. Transfer to a greased baking tray, making sure the seam is underneath. Brush all over with egg.

Use the pastry trimmings to decorate the coulibiac and make a small hole in the middle of the pastry to allow the steam to escape. Bake in a moderately hot oven (200 c, 400 f, gas 6) for about 30 minutes, or until golden brown and well puffed.

To serve, cut into thick slices and serve very hot with a bowl of chilled soured cream handed separately. Alternatively the coulibiac can be served cold with the cucumber and soured cream dip. **Serves 8**

Cabbage Filled with Dip

(Illustrated on pages 146/147)

300 ml/½ pint soured cream
1 tablespoon finely chopped radish
1 tablespoon finely chopped chives
150 ml/¼ pint mayonnaise
1 small cucumber, grated
100 g/4 oz salted cashew nuts, chopped

Mix the soured cream with the radish and chives, then stir in the mayonnaise. Squeeze out all the liquid from the cucumber – do this with your hands – then add the grated cucumber to the dip. Stir in the nuts and chill lightly.

Cut out the middle of a large cabbage and find a basin or bowl which will fit into the cavity. Leave the outer leaves of the cabbage to surround the bowl.

Spoon the dip into the bowl and place it in middle of the cabbage to serve. Complete the decoration, if you like, by inserting fresh flowers in between the leaves of the cabbage. **Serves 8**

Big Green Salad

A large, healthy green salad always goes down well at a party, but make sure that all the ingredients are shredded or chopped finely enough to be eaten without difficulty using just a fork.

Use crisp fresh lettuce (Iceberg, for example) or Chinese cabbage or endive. Add shredded spring onions, finely sliced green peppers, alfalfa or bean sprouts, strips of cucumber and sliced avocado pears. Any other green vegetables can be added.

Toss all the ingredients together in a large bowl, remembering to add the avocados at the last minute so that they won't have time to discolour. Serve your favourite dressing to accompany the salad or make a simple vinaigrette (page 61).

Tremendous Trifle

(Illustrated on pages 146/147)

FIRST LAYER
16 trifle sponges (2 packets)
300 ml/½ pint sherry, Cointreau, Kirsch or other liqueur
SECOND LAYER
1 kg/2 lb exotic fruit, peeled and stoned
(for example, kiwis, lychees and mangoes)
THIRD LAYER
900 ml/1½ pints milk · large vanilla pod
90 g/3½ oz caster sugar
6 teaspoons cornflour · 6 eggs
FOURTH LAYER
pared rind and juice of 3 lemons
350 ml/12 fl oz sherry or white wine
6 tablespoons brandy · 225 g/8 oz caster sugar
900 ml/1½ pints double cream
DECORATION
sugared almonds · kiwi slices
angelica strips

Line a very large dish with the trifle sponges and soak them in the sherry or liqueur. Cover these with the prepared fruit.

For the next layer, heat the milk with the vanilla pod in a large heavy-based saucepan. Mix the sugar with the cornflour and eggs. Pour on a little of the hot milk, stir well and pour the mixture into the saucepan with the rest of the milk. Stir constantly over a moderate heat until it thickens; do not boil. Strain, pour over the fruit and cool.

For the next layer, place the lemon rind and juice in a bowl with the sherry or wine and the brandy. Cover tightly and leave to stand while the custard is cooling. Strain this mixture, discard the lemon rind and mix the liquid with the sugar, stirring until it dissolves. Gradually stir in the cream, then whisk the mixture until it stands in soft peaks. Spoon this syllabub over the trifle. Decorate and chill. **Serves 30**

I am not married to a great chef or even an average chef — well, to be honest, my husband Bryan can't actually cook. However, one year he decided to burst upon the culinary stage with a Nureyev-like leap and produced a quite superb (if bankrupt-making) trifle which he has since repeated every Christmas, taking the rest of the year to work up to it! His first comment on hearing I was going to write this book was "Are you going to include The Trifle?" So, here it is: it is superb ... and he knows it!

Crafts

Once, when collecting Sarah from school, a teacher rushed up to her and said, 'Sarah, this button is off your uniform — you'd better get your mummy to sew it on again'. Sarah looked very worried and, to my horror, replied gravely, 'Oh dear, I hope mummy can manage it'. That teacher always gave me a strange look after that.

Of course I *can* sew a button on but it is true that my ability with a needle is limited. At school I learnt a hem stitch, and running stitch, and exasperation! While other girls appeared wearing skirts or blouses they had made, my efforts ended up as dusters. The same with knitting — I started to make Emma a matinee jacket when I was pregnant and two years later it was finally finished and given to her teddy. Even then it wasn't his 'best' outfit due to its odd shape; it was only for everyday.

So — as you can see — my skills in these areas are negligible. However, desperate to achieve something in this creative field, I have become very good at needlepoint (so have my daughters) and I can, believe it or not, make some Christmas presents. Perhaps because I wished I could knit or sew as a child, I wanted to give my children every opportunity to be creative. Although I couldn't help them to whip up outfits on the machine, or knit anything other than a scarf, we have cooked together, needlepointed, and just before Christmas we become like a mini factory. Enthusiasm is our great driving force (I now even possess a Black and Decker tool kit, so there's no holding me back) and we believe that home-made presents fall into two categories — horrendous or enchanting. I hope you will agree that the items on the following pages are simple to make; all you need is imagination to give a friend something that is personal, unique and — of course — enchanting.

TREE DECORATIONS

Bear

Following the pattern on pages 172/173, cut out two bear shapes from cotton material (or even better use an old piece of patchwork) allowing 5 mm/$\frac{1}{4}$in all the way round for a seam. Place the right sides of the material together and stitch neatly all the way round, 5 mm/$\frac{1}{4}$in. in from the edge. Remember to leave a small unstitched gap at the top of the bear's head (between the ears) so that the material can be turned right side out and stuffed.

When you have sewn round the shape, carefully snip in towards the stitching on all the corners and curved seams, then turn the bear right side outwards. Stuff the bear with kapok, making it chubby and cuddly. Make sure that the stuffing is pressed well into the paws and arms, then neatly stitch up the opening at the top of the head.

Cut out a small heart shape from a piece of red felt and stitch this on to the bear. Loop and neatly attach a piece of ribbon on the top of the bear's head so that he can be hung from the tree. To finish your bear, simply embroider two small eyes on the face, or sew on two small buttons if the bear is not going to be given to children. Tie a bow round his neck and the bear is ready to hang on the tree, or to be packed as a gift.

Potpourri Pig

This can be made of pink felt or any other suitable material. The pig is made in the same way as the bear: cut out two shapes following the pattern on pages 172/173, allowing room for a seam. Place the right sides of the material together and stitch neatly all round the shape, working 5 mm/$\frac{1}{4}$in. in from the edge and leaving a small gap in the stitching underneath where the stuffing can be put into the pig. Before turning the material right side out neatly snip in towards the stitching at all the corners and round all the curves.

When you have finished the stitching and trimming, press potpourri well into the legs and snout to make a plump pig. Neatly sew up the hole and embroider two small eyes on the face. To make a curly tail, cut a long narrow strip of pink material, fold it in half widthways (with the right side of the fabric facing inwards) and sew up the long edge, and across one end, to make a tube. Use a long knitting needle to turn the tube right side out, then place a pipe cleaner in it and sew up the open end. Neatly stitch the tail on the pig and curl it round. Attach a loop of ribbon to hang the pig on the tree.

Baby Bear

Following the pattern on pages 172/173, cut out two small bear shapes in pale brown felt, allowing 5 mm/$\frac{1}{4}$ in. extra for a seam. Cut out four pieces for paws and feet – use a contrasting colour for these – two tiny pieces for eyes and another tiny piece for the middle of the nose.

Place the main pieces together and stitch them neatly round the edge – it is best to hand stitch felt pieces on the right side. Remember to leave a small gap through which to stuff the bear, then push in the kapok, making sure that the filling is even. The bear must not be stuffed too full. Stick or stitch the paws and feet, nose and eyes on to the bear. Attach a loop of ribbon if the bear is to be hung on the tree, and tie a bow round his neck.

Christmas Cat

Cut out two cat shapes from suitable material or felt (follow the pattern on page 173 and allow 5 mm/$\frac{1}{4}$ in. for a seam). Cut out the tail in the same material. Place the right sides of the material together and neatly stitch round the shape, leaving a 5-mm/$\frac{1}{4}$-in seam at the edge. Remember to leave a small unstitched gap to allow for filling the cat, then carefully snip in towards the stitching at all the corners and round all the curves in the seams. Turn the cat right side out and fill it with kapok. Sew up the tail in the same way; turn it right side out and stuff it too, then neaten the holes left for stuffing and attach the tail to the back of the cat. Curve the tail round to the front and catch it on to the body with just a stitch or two.

Embroider the eyes and nose on the face of the cat and attach several pieces of heavy thread for whiskers. Attach a ribbon so that the cat can be hung on the tree.

Hobbyhorse

Following the pattern on pages 172/173, cut out two horse-head shapes in white felt. Cut out pink felt ears and a piece of lace for the mane. Place the large pieces of felt together, with the lace pinned into the seam, facing inwards to make the mane, then stitch neatly all round the shape of the head leaving the base open. Carefully snip the seam all round the curve, then turn the hobbyhorse right side out. Stuff the head and place a small knitting needle or wooden skewer in position for the stick, then sew up as neatly and securely as possible.

To finish the hobbyhorse, stitch the ears in place and attach ric-rac braiding for the reins. Stick or sew pieces of felt in place for the eyes and attach a loop of ribbon so that the hobbyhorse can hang on the tree.

Flying Angel

Following the pattern on pages 172/173, cut out the body and arm shapes in blue or white felt. Cut the wings from silver fabric or white felt and cut the face, hand and foot in pink felt. Cut two of each shape and sew them together neatly all round the edge; it is best to sew felt on the right side, then trim the seam as neatly as possible. When sewing the pieces together remember to leave a small gap to stuff the angel.

Stuff the angel lightly and attach yellow felt for hair. Cut out a red felt heart and hang this from the angel's hand with a piece of ribbon. Attach a ribbon to hang the angel from the tree. Dot the wings with glue and sprinkle a little glitter over them.

If you like, the angel can be made very simply by cutting out one piece of each shape in the appropriate felt, then cutting out cardboard shapes as backing. The felt pieces can be stuck to the cardboard and a piece of ribbon attached to hang the angel from the tree.

Patchwork Ball

This ball is particularly easy to make. Polystyrene balls are available from good craft shops and art shops. Choose one which is not too small – one which is about the size of an orange should be just right. Cut small pieces of pretty fabrics of complementary colours. Using a pair of scissors, and the sides of the blade, press the pieces of fabric into the ball, working all round each piece and pressing the edge in well to prevent it from fraying. When you have pressed one piece in, place a second piece of fabric next to it and press this in too. Keep the middle of the material flat as you push the edge into the polystyrene and continue until the ball is completely covered. The finished effect should be one of quilting. Lastly, push a loop of ribbon firmly into the top of the ball so that it can be hung on the Christmas tree.

Decorated Walnuts

Paint a few walnuts red and set them aside to dry. Cut out felt leaves in green and select a strong glue to stick these on top of the walnuts when the paint has dried. Stick a loop of ribbon firmly on top to hang the nuts from the tree.

TABLE DECORATIONS

Cone Tree

For this simple table decoration you will need a polystyrene cone (these are available from good craft shops and aritist's suppliers). Make sure that you have lots of nicely shaped fir cones that are not too big and some wire to attach them to the polystyrene. You will also need some ribbon – choose matching colours.

To assemble the tree, attach a piece of wire to the base of each fir cone and, starting at the top of the polystyrene, press in the cones until the whole 'tree' is completely covered. Add loops of ribbon – secured with wire and stuck between the cones – to decorate the tree.

Dried Flower Bouquets

Small bunches of dried flowers can look very attractive on a simply decorated table. Select flowers and grasses that are in good condition and tie them neatly into bouquets. Make a small slit in a doilie and push the stalks of a bouquet through. Bind the doilies in place with ribbons just underneath the flowers and add a bow. Do not make the posies look too fussy: try to retain the natural beauty of the flowers.

Decoration Dough

450 g/1 lb plain flour · 350 g/12 oz salt
350 ml/12 fl oz water

Put the flour and salt in a large bowl. Gradually add the water and mix it in by hand to make a pliable dough. Knead the dough for a few minutes then roll it out and cut out small badges, tags or shapes to hang on the Christmas tree (you can buy biscuit cutters in the shape of hearts, stars and Christmas trees). Remember to cut small holes in any which you plan to hang on the tree or wish to put a ribbon through. Alternatively, mould pieces of dough into the shape of animals or any other items you wish to make.

Place the shaped dough on baking trays and bake in a cool oven (150c, 300F, gas 3) for $1\frac{3}{4}$ hours. Cool completely on a wire rack.

If you want to decorate the shapes, then paint them when they are cold and leave the paint to dry before applying a coat of varnish.

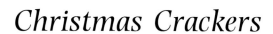

Christmas Crackers

Crackers made from material and decorated with old ribbons and lace make an outstanding addition to any Christmas table, tree or they can be used as a container for a small present. The crackers can also be made from paper: crepe and tissue paper, or any of the fine papers which can be obtained from specialist shops.

For an average-sized cracker the fabric or paper should be about 15 × 30 cm/6 × 2 in. in size (or larger if you wish). You will need some form of stiffening inside the crackers – loo paper rolls or kitchen rolls work well for this. For the fabric crackers use old lace, ribbon or small dried flowers as decoration.

Cut the material to size and cut the stiffening fabric slightly smaller. Lay the fabric right side downwards and place the lining on top. If you like you can have several layers of pretty fabrics cut to slightly different lengths so that each piece will show at the ends of the finished cracker. Mark the material into three sections: two ends each measuring just over a quarter of the total length of the fabric, and a central section which will be filled to make the body of the cracker (see diagram). Fold the materials in half lengthways, keeping them all together, so that the right side of the outer fabric is facing inwards. Pin and stitch the materials down the raw edge, then turn the right side out to make a tube. The middle section can be strengthened with a cardboard tube and filled with the chosen gifts. Search around antique shops before Christmas to find old bits of inexpensive jewellery or other small items which are suitable for putting into the crackers. Gather the material at the points marked on the cracker to make the decorative ends, then pull the gathering tight to close the middle section. Secure the gathering by tying a piece of ribbon round each end.

Trim the edges of the material with pinking shears and add some lace, ribbons, or flowers as trimmings – follow the ideas shown on those crackers which are illustrated in the pictures if you like.

Make paper crackers in the same way, using glue to stick the paper in place and using cardboard instead of the stiffening material. Decorate the crackers with cones, flowers, bows of ribbon and small toys if they are intended for children.

Note: Material crackers with written-out names attached make good place tags for the Christmas dinner table.

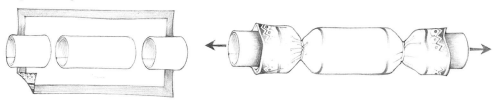

PRESENT-GIVING

Cat Cushion

For this you will need some suitable cotton fabric (or rescue a piece of an old patchwork bed cover). Following the pattern on page 174 cut out the shape of the cushion, head and tail, cutting each piece on a double thickness of material.

The fabric should be laid together with the right sides inwards and the cushion should be stitched neatly round the edge, leaving a 1-cm/$\frac{1}{2}$-in seam allowance and remembering to leave a small unstitched gap for stuffing. Sew the head in the same way and sew the tail pieces together.

Snip inwards towards the stitching all round the seam of the main cushion, head and tail, then turn all three with the right sides out. Stuff each piece fairly firmly, then sew up the openings. Position the head on the cushion and stitch it neatly in place. Similarly, position and attach the tail. Make sure that your stitching is hidden under the head and neatly under the end of the tail.

To finish the cushion either embroider the eyes or attach small buttons to the face. Add whiskers made of thread and a small embroidered nose.

Christmas Stocking

Following the pattern on page 174, cut out the stocking in red felt. Stitch the edges together, on the right side, with only a small seam allowance – about 5 mm/$\frac{1}{4}$ in – then bind the edges, if you like, with red satin ribbon. Trim the top of the stocking with several rows of lace and bows of red satin ribbon. Add, if you like, gold or silver bells and make sure that there is a loop of ribbon securely attached for hanging the stocking.

If you have time a patchwork stocking looks great.

Baby's First Christmas Bib

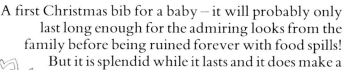

A first Christmas bib for a baby – it will probably only last long enough for the admiring looks from the family before being ruined forever with food spills! But it is splendid while it lasts and it does make a nice gift for a proud new mother.

Use one of baby's existing bibs as a pattern and cut out the shape in fine white material (or another delicate colour). Attach satin ribbons as ties and trim the bib with layers of lace in any pattern you choose.

On a piece of tissue paper, cut to the same size as the middle of the bib, write the words 'My First Christmas' then lay the paper over the bib and embroider the words in gold thread. When you have finished, simply remove the tissue to leave the embroidery in place.

Victorian Cushions and Pin Cushions

Gather as many bits of material, ribbons, old bits of lace, tray cloths and table mats as you possibly can. Start by cutting out the basic shape (round, heart shape, oblong or square) then appliqué pieces of lace or old material which you have gathered over the basic shape. For instance, start by stitching on a tray cloth (in the case of an oblong design) then add a table mat and bits of lace to make an attractive cover. Build up the design as you go, stitching each piece carefully before adding yet another layer. Mark out initials on a pin cushion using pins, or embroider them in gold thread. Make your cover lavish (it's one time when overkill looks great) whether it is a large item or a small pin cushion.

I made one for Shiela Attenborough. I embroidered very carefully the words 'The Year of Gandhi' only to discover that I had spelt Gandhi wrong and had to unpick it and start again.

Emma's Moles

To make these delightful moles you need modelling clay, the sort that dries on its own and doesn't need baking, varnish, water paints or poster colour paints and any decorative accessories for the moles you particularly want to make.

First make a basic cone shape of modelling clay, slightly larger than your thumbnail. Flatten and shape small pieces of clay to make arms and feet. Tuck the arms round the side of the body and stick the feet underneath the mole. Depending on what type of mole you are making add the necessary decoration: for a choir boy mole add a clay ruff round the neck, a song book in the hands and make a hole in the face to make a singing mouth (use the end of a paint brush to do this). Wait for the clay to dry before painting the moles.

Use your imagination and make as many different moles as you like – try some of the ideas illustrated here if you like.

I started to make these moles about two years ago, as a fun present for friends – I'm not exactly sure why I chose to make moles, but they are an extremely easy shape to mould, and I found that I could give each one its own character.

Emma

Needlepoint Cushion

Decide on the finished size of the cushion and cut a piece of squared paper to this size. Divide the canvas into as many squares as you would like, allowing a little room between each square for a line of contrasting stitching. Bind the edge with sticky tape or strong brown tape to prevent it from fraying. Work out your pattern: choose simple shapes or designs and use any of your favourite patterns. Work on just one square at a time. Decide on the colour scheme and select complementary colours; it is important to plan the colours as carefully as the pattern. Pick one colour to needlepoint between each square when you have finished the cushion.

When the needlepoint is finished, back the cover with a suitable fabric and use it to cover a plain white cushion. The finished canvas will need stretching in which case you will have to take it to a good craft shop to do this. If the novelty wears off before all the squares are finished, then make those which are completed into a pin cushion.

Needlepoint Cover

Cut a large piece of coarse cotton material, roughly following the dimensions given below. Cut a second piece of pretty material, about 5–7.5 cm/2–3 in bigger than the first piece. Lay this piece over the coarse cotton, placing the material right side upwards. Pin it in place all round the edge, then turn the whole thickness over and bring the edges of the pretty material over the backing. Fold the hem under and neaten the corners, then pin the material in place. Sew all round the hem, attaching the pretty fabric to the coarse backing and keeping the corners as tidy as possible.

Turn the cover over and attach a small square of pretty fabric in one corner, pressing a little kapok into it to make a small pin cushion. Arrange curtain rings along the top of the cover as shown, then stitch them securely in place. Turn the case over so that the coarse backing is showing, then attach two tapes roughly halfway up the case and towards one end of the fabric. These will be used for tying the case when it is filled with wools. If the tapes are stitched in place right in the middle of the cover you will not be able to roll the material neatly, so they should be positioned to one end.

The skeins of wool can be loosely knotted around the curtain rings, then the cover can be rolled and tied with the needlepoint in progress safely inside. I found this very useful for travelling.

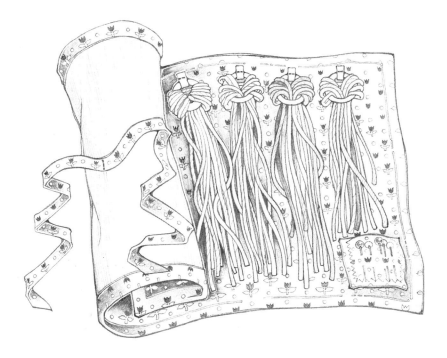

Christmas Cheating

Buy the very best Christmas pudding available and prick it all over with a skewer, then pour plenty of brandy or rum into it and wrap it tightly in cooking foil. If you have time repeat this process over a few days.

The best quality bought Christmas cake can be treated in the same way as the Christmas pudding. Turn the cake upside-down and pierce it all over with a skewer, then trickle plenty of brandy over the surface. Wrap the cake in cooking foil and repeat if you have time.

Shop bought mincemeat can be enlivened by adding brandy or rum and some grated orange or lemon rind. If you are really stuck for time, buy the best mince pies you can find. Carefully lift off their lids and spoon a little brandy over the filling. Serve home-made brandy or rum butter with the warmed pies.

If you don't have the time to prepare your own mayonnaise, then buy the best available and add a little double cream just as you are using it.

Simple casseroles can be varied and made more elaborate by adding interesting ingredients: try dried apricots, halved walnuts or shredded orange or lemon rind. You can freeze a simple meat or poultry casserole well in advance, then by adding something extra about 15 minutes before serving you can transform it into a nice meal just when you're in a panic.

Remember to freeze any dregs of wine by pouring it into ice-making trays. This way it will be ready for use in individual cubes for casseroles and sauces.

Frozen puff pastry can be improved to a high standard by rolling it out as thinly as possible, then brushing it with melted butter and folding it in half. Continue brushing the pastry with butter and folding it until it is about the same size as it was when you started, then roll it out for use.

Make a large batch of home-made tomato sauce (page 63) and keep it in the freezer – or even in the refrigerator for a few days. It is useful for a quick spaghetti, to have with meatloaf, to fill an omelette or to fill tiny pastry cases and bake for serving with drinks.

Opposite page Some hand-made presents: Needlepoint Cushion (page 161) with Cat Cushion (page 159) and Christmas Stocking (also page 159)
Overleaf Christmas crafts: Cone Tree, a child's picture, Sweet-topped Basket, Odds and Ends Presents, A Victorian Pin Cushion, Baby's First Christmas Bib, Christmas Crackers, Lavender Sachets, Dried Flower Bouquets and a Needlepoint Cover

A Few Ideas

Christmas eve, Christmas day, boxing day — or indeed on any special occasion — we all try to present something special, and particularly at Christmas. In my grandmother's house there was holly over the pictures and mirrors, a papier mâché Santa (brought out every year) with his sack full of sweets, mistletoe to giggle under, cards that were forever falling down, Advent calendars that were opened in surprise (even though we'd checked and opened every number and stuck it back) and bowls of nuts. Relatives and friends were welcomed in front of a blazing log fire, before which our night clothes would be hung in order to warm us up before we braved the chilly bedrooms.

When I was a child nobody used words like 'naff' or found it necessary to describe christmas decorations as 'kitsch'. Smart magazines hadn't decided whether celebrating Christmas was 'in' or 'out' and no one wondered whether it was good taste to have mistletoe over the door, no one questioned the ritual of high tea. In the absence of all these latter-day experts with their boring book of rules, no one cared. It was Christmas, it came but once a year, we were family, we had looked forward to it and now we were going to enjoy it. It was the extra attention to detail and the unusual ideas that always made the occasion.

Opposite page Nanette decorating the Christmas tree

Lace-trimmed Christmas Cards Look around antique shops and markets for old lace and Victorian Christmas cards. Carefully trim a pretty card with an edge of old lace, neatly glued in place.

Lavender Sachets Make small lace or material bags and fill them with lavender or potpourri. Gather them at the neck with a piece of ribbon, tied in a neat bow. These make lovely gifts and they can be hung on the tree over the Christmas season, then used to scent a drawer or cupboard all the year round.

Lavender-filled Tree Decorations Make the Baby Bear or Bear on page 154 and fill it with lavender instead of kapok. These can be used to hang on coat hangers, or in cupboards.

Child's Picture Frame a child's picture in a simple frame and trim it, if you like, with tiny sweets of different colours.

Odds and Ends Presents Cover the lid of a wooden box with lots of tiny throw-away bits and pieces – nuts, paper clips, pen tops, small spoons, buttons, cotton reels and any other bits you can fit on. Stick all the items on to the lid with strong glue then spray the whole arrangement in gold.

Home-made Preserves Cover pots of mincemeat, jam or marmalade with pretty fabric covers and label them with neatly written tags. These make a welcome gift, particularly for elderly people who live alone.

Cinnamon Bundles Tie bundles of cinnamon sticks with pieces of ribbon and decorate them extravagantly. Give them to a friend who enjoys cooking, or add them to the Christmas table.

Sweet-topped Basket Choose a firm, lidded basket and decorate the top with an arrangement of coloured sweets. Varnish the sweets and let the coating dry. You can also decorate a lidded jar in this way if you like.

Flower-filled Baskets Buy interesting old baskets from antique shops and markets and fill them with dried flowers (the prettiest you can find). Line the baskets, if you like, with old lace or some pretty material.

Present-wrapping Use your imagination when packing presents and follow some of the ideas shown in the photographs. Add tiny posies of dried flowers, decoration dough figures, sweets, silver and gold bells, and bows. Keep a spare, wrapped present handy with a spare tag, so that you can give a gift to an unexpected visitor without a last minute panic.

Doll's Christmas Tree Make a tiny tree for doll lovers, about 30 cm/ 12 in high. Cut a piece of polystyrene into a tree shape. Stick pieces of pine into it till it looks like a tree. Decorate the tree with doll's house things. Put in your child's room, with teddy bears round it.

Table Settings The exciting thing about the way you present food is that it gives you an opportunity to create your own style, to be different from everybody else. I always compare it to designing sets for a stage play – the audience (your guests) arrive, the curtain goes up, and the first pleasure is visual.

You can create a wonderful evening eating at a scrubbed table in the kitchen. Decorate the table with wild flowers in an old vase and candles, have a bowl of great soup, home-made bread, a bottle of wine and old friends. Or you can go all out for a more elaborate setting. Whichever you choose don't be dictated to by what is in or out of fashion or by what everybody else is doing. Entertain in the way that suits you – it doesn't take a lot of money, only imagination.

Pomander Balls Stick whole cloves into an orange, then roll it in a mixture of nutmeg, allspice, orris-root and cinnamon. Tie with ribbon.

Christmas Tree Ideas If you would like to have a tree but don't have the time or the inclination to decorate it, don't underestimate the beauty of an unadorned tree. Try and buy a variety that has a very lush look, and as near perfect a shape as possible. Just stand it in its pot (or put the pot in a basket). Alternatively, arrange three trees together in the hall or on a table. If you felt they were too plain for your liking, spray liberally with snow, or buy some gypsophila (baby's breath) and lay small clusters of it among the branches. It will look lovely.

Mirabelles Flambe This is a useful dessert for when you're in a tearing hurry. Drain the juice from a can of mirabelles or plums and pour it into a saucepan. Boil this syrup until lightly caramelised, then carefully pour in about 150 ml/$\frac{1}{4}$ pint cold water and heat gently until the caramel melts. Pour the caramel over the drained fruit (arranged in a heatproof serving dish) and pour over about 150 ml/$\frac{1}{4}$ pint brandy. Ignite immediately and serve while flaming.

Prunes in Armagnac and Apricots in Brandy For an easy-to-make, delicious gift, two-thirds fill sterilised jars with either dried prunes or apricots. Make a sugar syrup (about 100 g/4 oz sugar to 150 ml/$\frac{1}{4}$ pint water) and mix it with an equal volume of brandy. Bring to the boil, then pour the flavoured syrup over the fruit, making sure that the fruit is fully immersed. Cool, then seal tightly and attach a pretty label.

Templates for Tree Decorations and Gifts

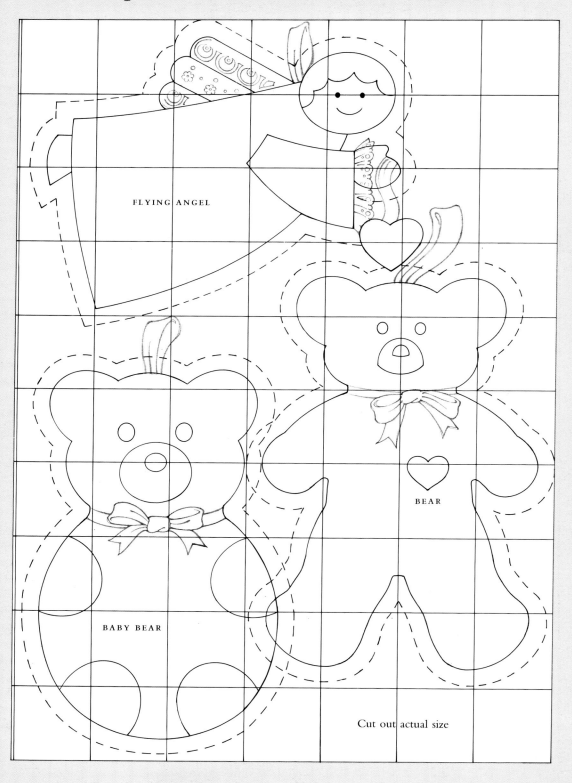

FLYING ANGEL

BEAR

BABY BEAR

Cut out actual size

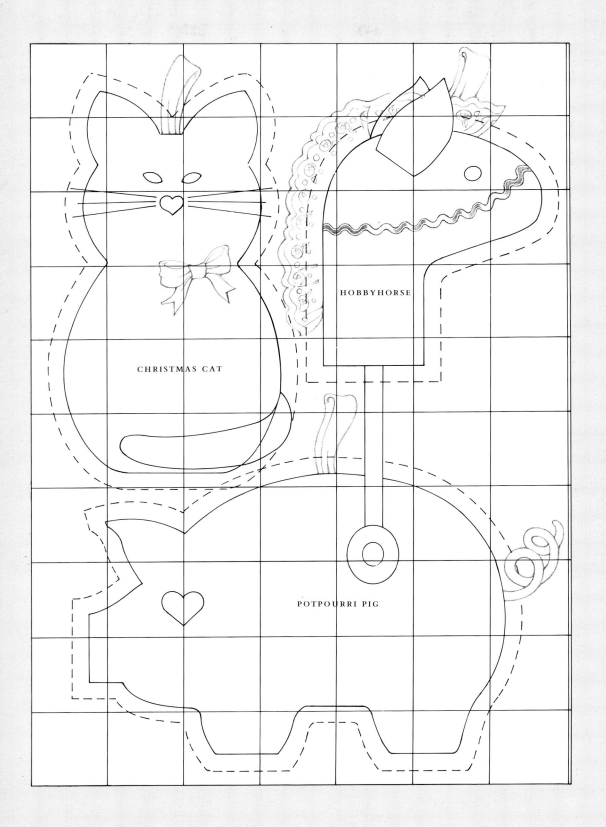

CHRISTMAS CAT

HOBBYHORSE

POTPOURRI PIG

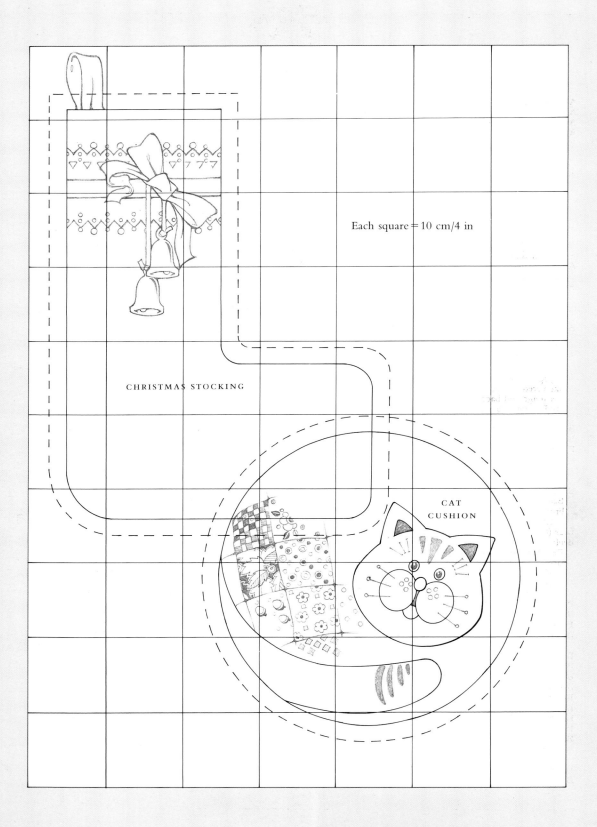

Each square = 10 cm/4 in

CHRISTMAS STOCKING

CAT
CUSHION

Index